ANTHOLOGY OF 20TH CENTURY
PIANO MUSIC

C000151897

Intermediate to Early Advanced Works b.

EDITED BY MAURICE HINSON

AN ALFRED MASTERWORK EDITION

Cover art: Courtesy of PlanetArt

ANTHOLOGY OF 20TH CENTURY PIANO MUSIC

EDITED BY MAURICE HINSON

Contents

This volume is dedicated to David Doscher,
with admiration and appreciation.

Maurice Hinson

Foreword:
The 20th Century

The 20th century saw the exploration of many styles and approaches to piano music, as well as a number of innovations. Composers ventured out in new directions and sought new sounds. Some composers introduced new harmonic principles that broke away from the harmonic systems of the past, while some embraced a more traditional framework (often with a fresh, new perspective).

The Romantic tradition, through European influence—especially from Germany's Franz Liszt (1811–1886), Johannes Brahms (1833–1897), Richard Wagner (1813–1883) and Gustav Mahler (1860–1911)—strongly affected America's 19th- and early-20th-century composers such as John Knowles Paine (1839–1906), Arthur W. Foote (1853–1937), George Chadwick (1854–1931), Amy Beach (1867–1944) and Edward MacDowell (1861–1908). French Impressionistic influence can be seen in the works of Charles Griffes (1884–1920). Later American composers such as Samuel Barber (1910–1981) and Virgil Thomson (1896–1989) were also influenced by the European Romantic tradition.

The music of another American, Charles Ives (1874–1954), remained virtually unknown for many years, even though Ives had completed two piano sonatas and a large number of shorter piano pieces and studies by 1920. Native American music attracted and influenced many American composers from around 1890–1920. Arthur Farwell (1872–1952) was among those inspired by this nationalistic influence.

Arnold Schoenberg (1874–1951) made his first attempts at atonal[1] music around 1908–1909 and evolved his system of 12-tone or serial technique[2] from 1921–1923.

Another style of 20th-century music, Neo-classicism, incorporated musical forms and characteristics of the 17th and 18th centuries. Neo-classicists Igor Stravinsky (1882–1971) and Paul Hindemith (1895–1963) had great influence on many

composers from approximately 1925 to 1950. Other composers influenced by Neo-classic ideals include Béla Bartók (1881–1945), Aaron Copland (1900–1990), Serge Prokofiev (1891–1953) and Erik Satie (1866–1925). These composers are represented in this collection.

More experimental composers such as Henry Cowell (1897–1965), Lou Harrison (1917–2003) and Emma Lou Diemer (b. 1927) used tone clusters to express their ideas.

Many 20th-century composers fused folk music with art music. Béla Bartók was one of the most successful composers to do this. His style was so greatly influenced by the folk music he collected (mainly from Central Europe) that his pieces are hard to discern from actual folk music. In addition to Bartók, other composers who used folk materials (also represented in this collection) include Aaron Copland, Ross Lee Finney (1906–1997), Alberto Ginastera (1916–1983), Percy Grainger (1882–1961), Nelson Keyes (1928–1987) and Heitor Villa-Lobos (1887–1959).

Jazz and ragtime elements were also of great influence in the 20th century. Copland used elements of jazz in his piece *Sentimental Melody*. The influence of ragtime on Satie and Claude Debussy (1862–1918) are represented in this collection by Satie's *Le Piccadilly* and Debussy's *Minstrels*.

Spanish and Latin-American influence is seen in *Tango* by Joaquín Turina (1882–1949), *Ritual Fire Dance* by Manuel de Falla (1876–1946), *Jamaican Rumba* by Arthur Benjamin (1893–1960) and *The Little Spaniard* by Ignacy Friedman (1882–1948).

The remainder of the composers represented in this anthology have developed their own unique voices, in which thematic integration and excellent craftsmanship are paramount.

I hope that piano teachers and piano students of the 21st century will enjoy and appreciate the wonderful musical pluralism of the previous century. This great era held some of the finest piano music ever written.

---

[1] Atonal: lacking a tonal center, with no feeling of key.

[2] 12-tone or serial technique: a compositional method using all 12 tones in a predetermined series.

About This Edition

Anthology of 20th Century Piano Music provides an up-to-date, comprehensive survey of piano music from the 20th century. It includes a variety of teaching repertoire, which has been selected to provide the widest range of styles and idioms from the period. Much of the music comes from the 20th century's best-known composers, but a few worthy works from lesser-known composers are also included. The works range in difficulty from the intermediate to the early-advanced level.

All pieces are in their original form and nothing has been added or deleted unless mentioned in footnotes. In some instances, selected pieces have been chosen from more lengthy works, a practice common during the 20th century.

This anthology is a performing edition. Brief discussions about the composers and music, history, performance problems and suggestions, along with the form of each piece, are presented in the section "About the Composers and the Music." All fingerings and pedal indications are editorial unless stated otherwise in footnotes. Editorial pedal has been added for the aid of students. More or less pedal than indicated can be used when playing these pieces. All parenthetical material is likewise editorial.

Suggested Further Reading

Burge, David. *Twentieth-Century Piano Music.* New York: Schirmer Books, 1990.

Cope, David H. *New Directions in Music.* Dubuque, IA: Wm. C. Brown, fourth edition, 1984.

Hinson, Maurice. *Guide to the Pianist's Repertoire.* Bloomington, IN: Indiana University Press, third edition, 2000.

Struble, John Warthen. *The History of American Classical Music.* New York: Facts on File, Inc., 1995.

Acknowledgments

Thanks to editors E. L. Lancaster, Carol Matz and Sharon Aaronson for their generous assistance and expert editorial advice, and to Linda Durkin for her superb administrative assistance.

About the Composers and the Music

BÉLA BARTÓK
(1881–1945)

This Hungarian composer was one of a handful of major composers of the 20th century. His style was influenced by the large number of folk songs he collected during his life. He was a marvelous pianist and his piano works mirror this great talent.

Bagatelle, Op. 6, No. 4; Sz. 38:4 17

Form: A = measures 1–2; A^1 = 3–4; B = 5–6; B^1 = 7–8; B = 9–10; B^1 = 11–12.

This piece is from a set of 14 *Bagatelles* composed in 1908. It is based on an old Hungarian folk song from the district west of the Danube. The words to this folk song are: "I was a cowherd and I slept by cows; I awoke in the night and not one beast was in the stall."

The key centers around the mode of D aeolian. Chordal textures vary from four to eight voices, requiring careful tonal balance. This piece also requires sensitivity to dynamic extremes, as well as quickness in moving from chord to chord. You may repeat the piece varying dynamics and pedaling.

Bear Dance, Sz. 39:10 18

Form: Theme and variations. A (theme) = measures 1–18; A^1 = 19–35; A^2 = 36–58; A^3 = 59–79; A^4 = 80–99; coda = 100–106.

This descriptive rhythmic study was composed in 1908. It centers around D and features a repeated-note ostinato with chords moving in parallel motion, dynamic surprises and accented bass notes. Hands must move quickly for chord preparation. Good facility in changing fingers on repeated notes is required. One should practice the piece much slower than suggested by Bartók's metronome marking, giving special attention to chordal balance.

Evening in the Country, Sz. 39:5 23

Form: A = measures 1–9; B = 10–20; A = 21–29; B = 30–41; A = 42–55.

Composed in 1908, this is one of Bartók's best-known pieces. Sections featuring a slow, expressive, free melody (measures 1–9, 21–29, 42–55) are contrasted with lively dance sections in strict rhythm (measures 10–20 and 30–41). It is an excellent piece for teaching different touches, as well as contrasting tempos and phrasing. Unlike many of Bartók's pieces, it is not based on a folk melody.

Romanian Folk Dances, Sz. 56 26

Bartók composed this set of six pieces in 1915, using seven different folk melodies.

Joc cu Bâtă (Stick Dance). Form: A = measures 1–8; A^1 = 8–16; B = 16–25; B^1 = 25–32; B^2 = 32–48.

According to Bartók, this dance is a "young men's solo dance, with various figures, the last of which—as a consummation—consists of kicking the room's ceiling."[3] The key centers around A with both dorian and aeolian modes used.

Brâul (Waistband Dance). Form: A = measures 1–4; B = 5–8; B^1 = 9–12; A^1 = 13–16.

Originally a folk flute solo, this melody centers around D in dorian mode. Delicate, graceful and poignant, this charming miniature requires careful phrasing and poetic feeling. It is also effective without pedal. This editor has suggested a change of dynamics on the repeat.

Pe loc (On the Spot). Form: Introduction = measures 1–3; A = 4–12; B = 12–20; C = 20–28; B^1 = 28–36; coda = 37–40.

This melody, also originally for flute, centers around B. In the original folk setting, the dancers remained in one location. Begin the inverted mordents on the beat, slightly accenting the first note.

Buciumeana (Dance of Butschum). Form: Introduction = measures 1–2; A = 3–6; A^1 = 7–10; B = 11–14; B^1 = 15–18.

Butschum is located in Transylvania, a region of Romania near the Hungarian border. This sensitive piece centers around A, mainly using the mode generated from the fifth degree of the harmonic minor scale. In measures 11–18, leaps in the left hand along with varied voicings require careful listening and a good feel for distance on the keyboard. Pedal is especially helpful for maintaining a legato left hand.

Poargă Românească (Romanian Polka). Form: Introduction = measures 1–4; part I = 5–16; part II = 17–28.

The tonal center of this piece alternates between D lydian and G lydian. Be careful of the tricky left-hand leaps (measures 11–16) and hand-crossing challenges (measures 20–22). The acciaccaturas (grace notes) and principal note combinations should be played almost simultaneously.

---

[3] David Yeomens, *Bartók for Piano* (Bloomington, IN: Indiana University Press, 1988), 75.

Măruntelul (Lively Dance). Form: **A** = measures 1–16; **B** = 17–24; **C** = 25–32; **B**¹ = 33–40; **C**¹ = 41–48; **C**² = 49–56; coda = 56–61.

Strong fingers, endurance, and facility in handling syncopated rhythms are required. The *Più allegro* section beginning in measure 17 is only a little faster than the opening *Allegro*.

Variations on a Slovakian Folk Tune, Sz. 42:II/5 .. 37

Form: Theme and variations.

This piece is based on a folk song, which contains the following text: "the peacock flew to his mother; play merrily, musicians, for my bridal wreath and golden ring are on the wall."

Variation I: The theme is in the left hand with right-hand counterpoint.

Variation II: The theme is in the right-hand with a left-hand chordal accompaniment.

Variation III: This variation contains a free canon between the hands in contrary motion, with a meter change from triple to duple.

ARTHUR BENJAMIN (1893–1960)

Arthur Benjamin was an Australian-born English composer. In his travels to Latin America (where he adjudicated for the Associated Board) he was exposed to music that made a lasting impression on him. He often wrote in a "light" style that is both delightful and uncomplicated.

Jamaican Rumba 40

Form: Introduction = measures 1–6; **A** = 6–22; **B** = 23–33; **A**¹ = 33–42; coda = 42–45.

This piece is Benjamin's best-known work. Originally composed in 1938 for two pianos, Benjamin subsequently created this arrangement for solo piano, as well as an orchestrated version. It features a light accompaniment with a bright rumba rhythm, along with a saucy melody and attractive counterpoint. Bring out the melody in the left hand beginning at measure 23.

LEONARD BERNSTEIN (1918–1990)

This celebrated American composer, conductor and pianist wrote in an eclectic style, blending elements of many types of music including jazz and Broadway. His writing is often syncopated and features strong rhythmic figures.

For Johnny Mehegan 43

Form: Built mainly around the opening idea (measures 1–2).

This piece is from *Four Anniversaries*, composed in 1945. It is a jazzy, syncopated scherzo that explores its opening idea throughout. Be sure to bring out the left hand in measures 14 and 24.

AARON COPLAND (1900–1990)

This great American composer's style is a blend of Neo-classic, folk and jazz elements. It has gradually and naturally evolved from the early French-inspired *Scherzo Humoristique* to the 12-tone *Piano Fantasy*. Copland composed numerous works, including ballets, orchestral works, chamber music and film scores.

In Evening Air 45

Form: Theme and variations. Introduction = measures 1–5; Var. I = 5–14; Var. II = 14–27; Var. III = 27–43; Var. IV = 44–59; coda = 60–65.

In Evening Air was composed in 1971. It requires a cantabile touch and tone balance in chord playing. Copland gives numerous character directions that help the pianist realize the mood.

Sentimental Melody 48

Form: Binary. Part I = measures 1–18; part II = 18–30.

This slow, jazzy dance was composed in 1929. It features bitonal writing and syncopated rhythms. The melodic line remains in the right hand. Be sure to convey a leisurely feel throughout the piece.

HENRY COWELL (1897–1965)

Around 1912, this American composer invented a new way of playing the piano—with arms, elbows and fists producing percussive chords called "tone clusters." A tone cluster comprises a dissonant group of adjacent tones sounded together. Cowell went on to compose many works in various styles throughout his productive career.

The Tides of Manaunaun 51

Form: Introduction = measures 1–2; through-composed[4] = 3–28; coda = 29–36.

Using the tone cluster technique, Cowell composed this piece around the age of 15. Be sure to read the "Explanation of Symbols" before beginning the piece. Notice that Cowell used a different key signature in each of the two staves of the grand staff. The composition builds to a gigantic climax (measures 22–25) before it subsides, matching the story given at the top of the piece. Try to bring out the top notes of the left-hand clusters in measures 22–23. At measure 24, be sure to roll the left-hand arpeggiated clusters slowly.

CLAUDE DEBUSSY (1862–1918)

This French composer was a seminal figure in 20-century music. He developed a keyboard style characterized by parallel chordal treatment, layers of sound, unresolved harmonies, unusual pedal effects, free modulations, and a full exploration of the piano's capabilities.

Danse de la poupée (The Doll's Dance), L. 128 . . . 54

Form: Ternary. Introduction = measures 1–12; **A** = 13–41; transition = 41–50; **B** = 51–72; **A**[1] = 73–88; coda = 89–101.

This piece is from Debussy's *La boîte à joujoux*, a "ballet for children," composed in 1913. In writing this music, Debussy endeavored (as he told his publisher), "to be clear and amusing without poses or pointless acrobatics."[5] It seems that Debussy was trying to recapture some of the spirit of his earlier *Children's Corner Suite*. The ballet was originally written for piano and later transcribed for orchestra by Maurice Ravel. Be sure that the opening arpeggiated chords in the right hand (measures 1–8), are played very crisply.

---

[4] Through-composed: music composed with no internal repetitions.

[5] Oscar Thompson, *Debussy: Man and Artist* (New York: Dover Publications, 1967), 358.

Minstrels, L. 117:12 58

Form: Five-part song. Part I = measures 1–34; part II = 34–44; part III = 45–57; part IV = 58–77; part V (coda) = 78–89.

Composed in 1910, this ragtime-inspired prelude comes from Book 1 of the *Préludes*. It is one of Debussy's most humorous pieces. The composition captures the atmosphere of the American minstrel show, which became popular in Europe at the turn of the 20th century. The piece is characterized by incisive ragtime rhythms and humorous mood alterations. A music hall character is established at the opening march, supported by a rhythmic staccato touch. Detached seconds (measures 9–10, 19–20 and 85–86) suggest the twang of a banjo. Measures 14–16 and 24–26 bring to mind the sound of trumpets. The drum is heard at measures 58–63.

EMMA LOU DIEMER (b. 1927)

American composer Emma Lou Diemer is an outstanding keyboard performer. She employs varied musical textures, and her energetic style displays masterly craftsmanship with a unique character.

Clusters and Dots 63

Form: Binary. Part I = measures 1–4; part II = 5–8; coda = 9–10.

Clusters and Dots is taken from a collection entitled *Sound Pictures*, composed in 1971. In this piece, one hand plays a cluster while the other hand has short, accented eighth notes. The coda contains clusters in both hands. Keep the rhythm very exact.

Gigue 64

Form: Binary. Part I = measures 1–15; part II = 16–37; coda = 38–46.

This playful piece features four-note chords in each hand plus a heavily accented melody. Be sure to bring out the left hand at measures 17–23.

Serenade 66

Form: Binary. Part I = measures 1–20; part II = 21–36.

This piece features singing melodies accompanied by repetitive rhythmic figures. These figures accentuate the irregular $\frac{5}{4}$ time signature. Be sure the left-hand melody is brought out in measures 12–16, 22–26 and 31–32.

MANUEL DE FALLA (1876–1946)

The piano was this Spanish composer's instrument, and it became a vehicle for some profound compositional statements. De Falla studied piano in Madrid with José Tragó (1856–1934) and composition with the powerful nationalist composer Filipe Pedrell (1841–1922), who strongly affected his compositional style.

Ritual Fire Dance 68

Form: Introduction = measures 1–23; **A** = 24–58; bridge = 59–66; **B** = 67–135; introduction = 136–155; **A** = 156–190; bridge = 191–198; **B** = 199–244; coda = 245–273.

This piece is from the ballet *El amor brujo* (Love, the Sorcerer), composed during 1914–15. De Falla created this piano arrangement from the orchestral score. The music is from the scene in the ballet in which Candelas, the main female character, dances at midnight to chase away all evil spirits. The piece is full of strong rhythms, trills, fast octaves in alternating hands and full chords in both hands.

ARTHUR FARWELL (1872–1952)

A great champion of American music, Farwell was at his best working with Native American material.

Approach of the Thunder God 76

Form: Binary. Part I = measures 1–9; part II = 10–15.

This piece is an original Native American melody, harmonized by Farwell. Be sure to project the melody throughout, even when supported by full chords. Take plenty of time to ensure that the 16th notes do not sound rushed. This editor suggests that the piece may be repeated with different dynamics; end strongly (*f*).

ROSS LEE FINNEY (1906–1997)

This American composer's early works had their roots in our American heritage. During the 1950s, Finney's tonal language became more chromatic and dissonant, eventually making use of serial technique.

Medley—Campfire on the Ice. 77

Form: **A** = measures 1–16; **B** = 16–40; **A**^{1} = 40–53.

In composing *Medley*, Finney dipped into a pair of American folk tunes ("Red River Valley" and "Dinah, Won't You Blow Your Horn?"). When the melodies are combined (measure 41 forward), the pianist must be sure to bring out both. Other performance challenges include passing the melody between hands and adjusting to sudden tempo changes.

CARLISLE FLOYD (b. 1926)

This American composer wrote in an eclectic but conservative style. All of his works are extremely well crafted, and many feature quartal harmonies, parallel fifths and chromaticism.

The following four pieces by Carlisle Floyd are all taken from *Episodes*, a 15-piece set composed in 1965.

Chorale 80

Form: Binary. Part I = measures 1–8; part II = 9–16; coda = 17–19.

The melodic line is located in the top voice. Be sure to observe the crescendo from measures 9–16.

Fourth Lyric Piece 81

Form: Ternary. Part I = measures 1–8; part II = 8–16; part III = 17–23; coda = 24–26.

This flowing right-hand melody is accompanied by syncopated left-hand chords in a mildly contemporary idiom.

Night Song 82

Form: Binary. Part I = measures 1–23; part II = 24–36.

This piece is a lovely and tender nocturne. The melody lies in the right hand. Be sure the final chord in measure 36 is softer than measure 35.

Waltz 84

Form: Binary. Part I = measures 1–21 (**A** = 1–9; **B** = 9–21); part II = 22–43 (**A** = 22–31; **B** = 32–43).

This sad miniature waltz is somewhat reminiscent of Chopin's *Waltz in A Minor*, Op. 34, No. 2. Be sure to bring out the melody, which remains in the left hand most of the time.

IGNACY FRIEDMAN (1882–1948)

Hailing from Poland, Ignacy Friedman was one of the 20th century's greatest pianists. He composed approximately 100 piano pieces of startling originality.

The Little Spaniard, Op. 76, No. 7 86

Form: Introduction = measures 1–4; **A** = 5–20; **A**^{1} = 21–36; **B** = 37–57; coda = 58–60.

This composition is from a set of eight pieces entitled *Vignettes*. Be sure that the 16th note in the left hand is not played as a triplet. Notice the two dynamic levels indicated in measure 5; the top voice (melody) is to be brought out over the middle voice.

ALBERTO GINASTERA (1916–1983)

This Argentinean composer's early works were in an essentially nationalistic style that made use of strong rhythms and South American folk music. He later moved toward atonal expressionism.

Rondo on Argentine Children's Folk Tunes 88

Form: **A** = measures 1–33; **B** = 34–55; bridge = 56–66; **A**^{1} = 66–91; **C** = 92–106; **A**^{2} = 107–123; coda = 124–133.

Composed in 1947 for Ginastera's children, this exciting piece juxtaposes Argentinean folk tunes with rousing accompaniments. Careful attention to tempo changes is required. Play the glissando in measures 115–116 with the thumb of the left hand. The final two measures should be forceful with a crashing sonority on the last chord.

PERCY GRAINGER (1882–1961)

Born in Australia, Grainger came to the United States in 1914 and became a citizen in 1918. He was an outstanding pianist, but is best known for his fresh and highly pianistic arrangements of English songs and dances.

Grainger's colorful performance directions have been retained in the following two arrangements. Voicing is very important since much of their melodies are given to inner voices.

Irish Tune from County Derry 93

Form: Song form. Verse 1 = measures 1–16; verse 2 = 16–32.

This is the tune for the familiar song "Danny Boy." Grainger arranged this tune for solo piano between 1902 and 1911. The melody, printed in large notes, is to be "well to the fore," or brought out.

The Sussex Mummer's Christmas Carol 96

Form: Song form. Verse 1 = measures 1–11; verse 2 = 11–22.

Grainger arranged this tune for solo piano between 1905 and 1911 and dedicated it to the memory of Edvard Grieg, his close friend. A mummer is a masked and costumed actor in the rural plays traditionally performed throughout England at Christmas time.

CHARLES GRIFFES (1884–1920)

Charles Griffes, an American, had a great love for Asian subjects and was preoccupied with Impressionist techniques.

The Lake at Evening, Op. 5, No. 1 104

Form: Introduction = measures 1–2; **A** = 3–23; **B** = 24–45; **A**^{1} = 46–61; coda = 61–67.

This piece is one of *Three Tone Poems*, Op. 5, composed between 1910 and 1912. Griffes included an epigraph at the beginning of each piece. The one used here, from *The Lake Isle of Innisfree* by William Butler Yeats (1865–1939), refers to "lake water lapping with low sounds by the shore..." This compelling piece has an eerie quality, produced by the insistent repetition of a rhythmic figure (ostinato) throughout, suggesting the lapping lake water. Be sure that the ostinato remains in the background. Bring out the melody in the right hand until measure 57, where it shifts to the left hand.

The White Peacock, Op. 7, No. 1 98

Form: Introduction = measures 1–7; **A** = 7–17; **B** = 17–26; **C** = 26–50 (development); **A**^{1} = 50–60; coda = 60–66.

This piece was composed in 1915 and published in 1917 as part of four *Roman Sketches*, Op. 7. The idea of *The White Peacock* was suggested as early as 1903 when Griffes visited a zoo in Berlin. Griffes was also inspired by a poem of the same title from *Sospisi de Roma* (Roman Sketches, 1891) by the mystic Scottish-Celt poet William Sharp (1855–1905) who wrote under the literary name of Fiona Macleod. For most of the piece, the use of flat fingers is recommended for maximum control of key descent. Maintain a very good legato throughout.

LOU HARRISON (1917–2003)

This American composer's music encompasses a wide range of styles—from virtually primitive to light and pleasant; from exotic Eastern-influenced pieces to serious 12-tone composition.

Form: Rondo. A = measures 1–8; A^1 = 8–16; B = 16–26; A^2 = 26–34; C = 34–44; A^1 = 44–52; D = 52–63; A^1 = 63–71; C = 71–81; A^2 = 81–89.

Lou Harrison studied with Henry Cowell from 1934–35. This piece by Harrison, with its many tone clusters, clearly shows Cowell's influence. *Reel* features right-hand clusters interspersed with an active single-line melody over ostinato-like figures in the left hand. The Irish-style tune is treated with all black keys in the right hand, and mostly white keys in the left hand.

JACQUES IBERT (1890–1962)

French composer Jacques Ibert composed ballets, chamber and piano music, operas, songs, and symphonic poems. His polished writing displays characteristics of Neo-classical and Impressionistic styles and is frequently witty and light.

Form: A = measures 1–8; B = 9–18 using material from the A section in different keys; A^1 = 19–30 similar to the A section with left-hand chromatic figuration in measures 19–20 and 23–25.

This piece comes from the collection of 10 pieces entitled *Histoires* (Stories) composed in 1922. This fickle "giddy girl" is unable to decide if she loves her boyfriend or not! Her changeable emotions are portrayed through the numerous tempo and character changes. A fairly light touch is appropriate throughout this piece. Bring out the duet lines between the tenor voice and top line in measures 3–4, 7–8 and 21–22.

NELSON KEYES (1928–1987)

This American composer wrote in an eclectic idiom, but was at his best working with American folk material. Keyes wrote these three pieces as a birthday gift for his pianist wife.

Gently, Johnny, My Jingalo. Form: A = measures 1–15; A^1 = 15–27; A^2 = 27–40; A^3 = 40–54; coda = 54–55.

The melody is treated canonically in measures 40–54; be sure that the tune is heard throughout.

Shenandoah. Form: A = measures 1–10; A^1 = 10–20; coda = 20–24.

This piece features an expressive melody and changing meters. The legato sixths in the left-hand part must flow with great ease.

Lolly-Too-Dum. Form: Introduction = measures 1–4; A = 4–30; A^1 = 30–56; bridge = 56–61; B = 62–88; A^1 = 89–119; coda = 119–126.

This piece contains an open-fifth accompaniment, bitonality and more development than in the other two songs in the set. Canonic treatment between the hands in measures 89–104 requires careful tonal balance.

ZOLTÁN KODÁLY (1882–1967)

Kodály's style is mainly melodic and related to the Hungarian folk idiom. His structures are always clear and well proportioned.

Form: Rondo. A = measures 1–8; B = 9–16; C = 16–24; A^1 = 24–32; A^2 = 33–39; D = 40–44; A^3 = 45–56.

This piece is played on the black keys throughout (indicated by the large sharps at the beginning of the piece). Pay careful attention to articulation and tied notes.

BENJAMIN LEES (b. 1924)

American composer Benjamin Lees mixes polyphonic textures with classic forms in a thoroughly contemporary idiom.

No. 9. Form: Binary. Part I = measures 1–21; part II = 22–36.

This strong march contains intriguing tonal sonorities mixed with changing meters. It contains a minimum of textural contrast. Be sure to distinguish between accents and tenuto marks.

No. 10. Form: **A** = measures 1–14; **B** = 14–26; **C** = 27–41; **A**^{1} = 42–58.

This fresh-sounding piece mainly exhibits perpetual motion. It contains some explosive octaves at measures 20–24, 47–53 and 57–58. Be sure to bring out the melody (in the left hand at measures 3–13, in the right hand at measures 15–25, then in the left hand again at measures 44–53).

BOHUSLAV MARTINŮ (1890–1959)

Czech folk songs, modality and rhythmic zest are all fused in the music of this Czech composer. The following three pieces come from a collection entitled *Puppets,* begun in 1912.

Form: **A** = measures 1–18; **B** = 19–42; **A** = 43–65.

This piece is a very graceful, charming waltz. The **B** section is a little faster than the **A** section.

Form: **A** = measures 1–12; **B** = 13–22; **A** = 22–34.

The shimmy was a dance that was popular in the United States in the 1910s and 1920s. Characteristics of this dance included moving the shoulders in opposite directions, forward and then backward. Be sure to bring out the melody in the alto voice in measures 2–4 and 23–25.

Form: **A** = measures 1–23; **B** = 24–41; **A** = 1–23.

This shy doll's character is "sweetly tranquil" in the **A** sections, but becomes quite active in the **B** section. Be sure to rest for the full value in measure 41.

DARIUS MILHAUD (1892–1974)

The French composer Darius Milhaud produced a large amount of varied works including operas and ballets, symphonies and other orchestral music, concertos, chamber music and piano pieces. His fluent style often features bitonality.

Form: Introduction = measures 1–4; **A** = 5–20; **B** = 21–36; bridge = 37–42; **A** = 43–58.

This piece is from a dance suite entitled *Saudades do Brazil* (Recollections of Brazil), completed in 1921. Each of the 12 poetic dances in the suite is named for a district of the city of Rio de Janeiro and reflects the unusual charms of each municipality. Observe the double-stemmed left-hand notes fastidiously as these provide the necessary finger pedals. At measures 18 and 56, arpeggiate the right-hand tenths from bottom to top. Keep a light touch with rhythmic clarity throughout so the tango rhythm can sparkle.

FRANCIS POULENC (1899–1963)

Francis Poulenc's style combines classical clarity with a talent for satire and caricature. Some of his inspiration came from Parisian street musicians, popular music halls (where popular music was performed) and circus bands. Poulenc's spontaneous melodic writing is one of his unique and easily identifiable qualities.

The *Mouvements perpétuels* were composed in October 1918. The lack of key signatures in all three pieces gives Poulenc the freedom to move through various keys without being restricted to any one key.

No. 1. Form: **A** = measures 1–11; **B** = 12–19; coda = 20–24 (built on **A**).

The repeating one-measure bass pattern creates a static harmony under a flowing melodic line. The direction *En général, sans nuances* (in general, without nuances) in measure 1 suggests a straightforward type of interpretation, especially as it relates to dynamics. Be sure to project the melody over the other voices.

No. 2. Form: **A** = measures 1–6; **B** = 7–12; coda = 13–14.

Although no key signature is indicated, the constant use of B-flat suggests the key of D minor (natural form), especially in the right hand. The word *indifférent* in measure 1 means both hands are to be played equally, at the same dynamic level, but the different phrasing in each hand must be observed. In measure 11, *2 Pedales* (Poulenc's indication) means to use both the damper and *una corda* pedals.

No. 3. Form: Introduction = measures 1–3; **A** = 4–7; **B** = 8–36; introduction = 37–39; **C** = 40–46; **C**^{1} = 47–50; coda = 51–57.

This movement contains more meter changes than the first two movements. The melody must always be heard over the accompaniment, even though part of the accompaniment is in the right hand with the melody. If the left-hand tenths (measures 1, 3 and similar places) must be broken, play the low note before the beat and the top note on the beat.

ANDRÉ PREVIN (b. 1929)

Previn is an American composer, pianist and conductor who was born in Germany. Although best known as a conductor, he has composed music in a variety of styles.

February 15 148

This piece is from a collection entitled *Five Pages from My Calendar*, in which the pieces represent the birthdays of Previn's children.

Form: **A** = measures 1–34 (part I = 1–16; part II = 17–34); **B** = 35–42; **A**^{1} = 43–63.

This piece is quite chromatic and moves through various tonal levels, while beginning and ending in D major. The melody remains in the top voice although there are places where the inner voice needs to be brought out (measure 51, for example).

SERGE PROKOFIEV (1891–1953)

The Russian composer Prokofiev developed a percussive style that could be considered the most significant innovation in piano technique since Chopin. His percussive manner of treating the piano is uniquely blended with lyricism, often accompanied by strong dissonance.

Prelude in C Major ("Harp"), Op. 12, No. 7 152

Form: **A** = measures 1–27; **B** = 27–54; **A** = 55–80; coda = 80–81.

The **A** section requires a quiet performance of the broken-chord figuration and careful voicing of the left-hand melody. The contrasting **B** section contains a percussive touch and graceful

pp glissandos. Note the Neo-classic influence.

Visions Fugitives (Fleeting Visions),

Op. 22, Nos. 1 and 5 158

The title of this set of 20 short pieces comes from the Russian poet Konstantin Balmont (1867–1942): "In every fleeting vision I see worlds full of the changing plays of rainbow hues."

No. 1. Form: **A** = measures 1–13; **A**^{1} = 14–27.

This piece is quiet and ethereal throughout. The *ppp* chords in measures 9–11 and 22–24 require careful tonal control.

No. 5. Form: **A** = measures 1–7; **B** = 8–11; **C** = 12–19.

This humorous piece uses polytonality (measures 12–18), syncopation (measures 10–11), and leaps (measures 3–7) to create a fun, witty feeling.

MAURICE RAVEL (1875–1937)

The piano music of this French composer is characterized by precise attention to detail, sharp outlines, and clear forms. His harmonies usually play a subordinate role to line and rhythm. A Classicist with Romantic tendencies, Ravel extended the pianistic traditions of Franz Liszt.

À la manière de Borodin

(In the Style of Borodin)—Valse. 160

Form: Binary. **A** = measures 1–32; **B** = 33–69; coda = 70–93.

Ravel used parody technique (the caricaturing of a composer's style) to write this piece in 1913. The **B** section (measures 33–69) contains an ornamented chromatic melody that is reminiscent of Borodin's *Polovtsian Dances* from the opera *Prince Igor*. This composition, with its colorful harmonies, demonstrates Ravel's ability to integrate and reproduce the styles of others. This is a flowing waltz that is both charming and capricious. Bring out the left-hand melody at measures 82–90.

Prélude 164

Form: **A** = measures 1–9; **B** = 10–15; **C** = 14–25; coda = 25–27.

This charming piece was composed in 1913 as a sight-reading piece for the Conservatoire de Paris piano competitions. A fine performance requires a good combination of relaxed tempo and expressiveness.

VLADIMIR REBIKOV (1866–1920)

Influenced by Debussy, this Russian composer experimented with whole-tone harmony. He also explored unresolved dissonance and novel forms.

Form: **A** = measures 1–10; **B** = 10–18; **C** = 19–31; **A**^{1} = 32–43; coda = 44–47.

These impish fiends seem to be having a great time romping through the whole-tone scale. Be careful to observe the dynamics in measures 1–5, 6–9, 32–35 and 36–39. This pianistic piece fits the hands beautifully.

Form: **A** = measures 1–8; **B** = 9–16; **A**^{1} = 17–24; **C** = 25–32; **A**^{2} = 33–44.

This mournful piece has a beautiful melody that must always be brought out. Focus on the lovely tenor-voice counterpoint in measures 17–24 and 33–36.

WALLINGFORD RIEGGER (1885–1961)

Riegger, an American, began composing in a 19th-century style, but later, under the influence of Schoenberg, became more adventurous. Characteristics of his later style include atonality, strong rhythmic treatment and contrapuntal forms. All three pieces included here come from a collection entitled *New and Old*, Op. 38, which illustrates Riegger's contemporary compositional techniques.

Form: **A** = measures 1–5; **B** = 6–9; **C** = 10–13; **D** = 14–21.

This piece is based on the B-flat augmented triad. It contains plenty of rhythmic drive and imitation between the hands.

Form: **A** = measures 1–4; **B** = 5–8; **C** = 9–12; **D** = 13–16.

This piece is based on two pairs of major seconds alternating between the hands. Dynamic contrast, change of register and different rhythmic groupings provide plenty of variety.

Form: **A** = measures 1–8; **B** = 9–20; **C** = 21–29.

The term "tritone" here refers to a succession of three whole tones, the basis for this piece. No pedal is to be used.

ERIK SATIE (1866–1925)

This Frenchman was one of the most original composers. He parodied styles of well-known composers, quoted from their works, and deliberately attached comical names to his pieces. Satie's writing contains fresh harmonies and simple melodies, completely avoiding any type of complexity.

Form: **A** = 1–24; **B** = 25–44; **A** = 1–24.

Composed in 1904, this piece is one of the earliest examples of the influence of jazz on European art music. Emphasize the catchy rhythms and keep the textures lean by very little use of the pedal. This work might have inspired Debussy's *Golliwogg's Cakewalk*.

Composed in 1917, this piece is a clever parody of Clementi's *Sonatina in C Major*, Op. 36, No. 1. *Sonatine bureaucratique* follows the Clementi work closely in its general structure and even includes some of its melodic material. In the score, Satie included satirical text relating to an office worker. (However, the words are not intended to be read during the musical performance.)

Allegro. Form: Sonata-allegro. Exposition = measures 1–23; development = 24–35; recapitulation = 36–54; coda = 54–58.

Observe the contrasting articulation throughout the movement. At measures 26–27 and 54–57, Satie introduces his own brand of humor using harmonic distortion.

Andante. Form: **A** = measures 1–8; **B** = 9–16; **A**^{1} = 17–22.

With their contrasting phrase structures, the left- and right-hand parts function like a duet through most of the movement.

Vivace. Form: Rondo. **A** = measures 1–16; **B** = 17–24; bridge = 25–28; **C** = 29–40; **D** = 41–52; **A** = 53–68; **B** = 69–76; bridge = 77–80; **C** = 81–92; coda = 93–116.

Bring out the left hand at measures 9–16 and 61–68. Use little pedal and keep the chords generally light.

ARNOLD SCHOENBERG (1874–1951)

The piano works of this Austrian-born composer are among the most significant contributions to the repertoire. His keyboard style stresses wide-interval melodies, subtle rhythmic usage, and sonorities that require the most careful balancing of parts. Shortly after World War I, Schoenberg began to form his theories concerning "12-tone" composition, marking the beginning of a new creative period.

Six Little Piano Pieces, Op. 19, Nos. 2 and 6 183

This set, composed in 1911, is the least complex of Schoenberg's piano works. These miniatures are subtle, fleeting sketches.

No. 2. Form: The form follows the partial tone row (9 tones) of G, B, D, F-sharp, D-sharp, A, C, A-flat and B-flat through measure 5; the A and C-sharp (interval of a third) in measure 6; then the partial row (11 tones) of C, E-flat, D, B, F-sharp, F, G, A, D-flat, E, and B-flat.

The piece contains fast-changing dynamics and centers around G with the repeated, opening left-hand thirds. These thirds are like a dripping faucet. The *ben ritmato* and *poco ritardando* indications (measures 7 and 9) suggest the subtlety of the closing measures.

No. 6. Form: The form follows the 12-tone row of A, F-sharp, B, G, C, F, D-sharp, E, B-flat, D, G-sharp and C-sharp through measure 7; then a partial row (11 tones) of D, F-sharp, E-flat, B, E, G-sharp, C, B-flat, G, F and A to complete the piece.

The composition ends with the opening chord along with a gesture in the lower register (B-flat to A-flat). Be aware of the extremely soft dynamics (*pp* to *pppp*).

CYRIL SCOTT (1879–1970)

Scott, an English composer, wrote many short piano pieces in an Impressionist style. This earned him the nickname of "The English Debussy."

Lento, Op. 35, No. 1 185

Form: **A** = measures 1–17; **B** = 18–27; **A**¹ = 28–36; coda = 37–41.

Lento is taken from *Two Pierrot Pieces*. Be sure that your fingers remain very close to the keys. Careful use of the pedal is required. Numerous left-hand chords will have to be arpeggiated (measures 3–4, 6, 11–14, etc.). This piece requires plenty of breathing space so that the listener can enjoy the rich harmonies.

IGOR STRAVINSKY (1882–1971)

This Russian-born composer is considered to be one of the greatest composers of the 20th century. His music exhibits great rhythmic interest. A sense of the theater and dance permeates his works.

The following three pieces by Stravinsky are taken from a set entitled *The Five Fingers*, composed near Paris in 1920–21. These pieces keep the right hand in the same place (over 5 keys) while the left hand performs very simple patterns.

Siciliana 188

Form: **A** = measures 1–14; **B** = 15–29.

Throughout the piece, the right hand uses only the notes D, E, F-sharp, G and A. Observe the accent marks in measures 17 and 19, and the tenuto marks in measure 20.

Lento 189

Form: **A** = measures 1–9; **B** = 9–13; **A**¹ = 13–19.

The right hand uses the following notes: measures 1–8 = D, E, F-sharp, G and A; measures 9–13 = F, G, A, B-flat and C; measures 13–19 use the opening set of notes. Notice that all the F's in the left hand are natural.

Pesante 190

Form: **A** = measures 1–9; **B** = 10–20; **A**¹ = 20–29.

Pesante means weighty, with emphasis. Numerous meter changes add to the interest of this piece. The right hand uses the following notes: measures 1–9 = B, C, D, E, F and F-sharp; measure 10 = B, C-sharp, E and G; measures 11–20 = C-sharp, D, E, F and G; measures 20–29 = B, C, D, E, E-flat and F.

KAROL SZYMANOWSKI (1882–1937)

Chopin, Scriabin, Richard Strauss, Debussy and Stravinsky all influenced this Polish composer, and yet he was quite an original.

Prelude in B Minor, Op. 1, No. 1 192

Form: Introduction = measures 1–3; **A** = 4–17; **A**¹ = 18–35; **B** = 36–52; coda = 53–59.

This piece is from a set of *Nine Preludes* composed between 1900 and 1902. It is somewhat chromatic and mainly shows the influences of Chopin and Scriabin. At measures 4–35, be sure to give full value to the notes of the melodic line. Push ahead a little at measures 36–43 (*poco agitato*).

ALEXANDER TCHEREPNIN (1899–1977)

Born in Russia, Tcherepnin became an internationally successful composer. He wrote in a spirited style, influenced by Asian and Georgian folk music.

Ten Bagatelles, Op. 5, Nos. 1 and 9 194

These pieces are from a set of *Ten Bagatelles* composed between 1913 and 1918.

No. 1. Form: **A** = measures 1–5; **B** = 5–9; **A** = 10–14; coda = 14–17.

The march-like quality of this bagatelle (a short, simple piece) is brought about by the use of various strong articulations. Here, the accent (>) is stronger than the staccatissimo (ᵛ). Keep a steady tempo.

No. 9. Form: Introduction = measures 1–4; **A** = 5–19; **B** = 20–43; **A** = 44–58.

Feel the tempo "one beat to the measure." Carefully observe the occasional tenuto marks. You may add touches of pedal at measures 5, 41 and 44 for added interest.

VIRGIL THOMSON (1896–1989)

This American composer wrote many musical "portraits" of his friends; the subjects sat for him (as for a painter) while he composed. The style of the works varied with the subject: dissonant, tuneful, harmonious, and/or contrapuntal. Stravinsky and Satie were major influences on Thomson's writing.

Homage to Marya Freund and to the Harp 198

Form: Bipartite. Part I = measures 1–16; part II = 17–31.

This piece is from a collection entitled *Thirteen Portraits*. According to Thomson's notes in the score, "Marya Freund, Polish-born soprano of Vienna and Paris, interpreted modern music and taught singing well into her late 80s." The arpeggiated chords suggest the harp; roll quickly, beginning the arpeggio with both hands simultaneously.

Sam Byers: With Joy 200

Form: Bipartite. Part I = measures 1–8; part II = 9–17.

This piece is from a collection entitled *Nineteen Portraits*. Thomson wrote in his score, "Sam Byers, young {man} from Missouri in the advertising business, {is} a fine regional cook." The piece begins and ends in choral style with flowing counterpoint in the left hand. Pay close attention to the articulation and to the various touches. In the opening and closing measures, legato and staccato touches are used simultaneously.

JOAQUÍN TURINA (1882–1949)

Having spent some time in France, this Spanish composer was influenced by Impressionism. Most of his piano works are written in somewhat popular styles. They are always colorful and exhibit a fine mastery of form.

Tango, Op. 8, No. 2 201

This piece is from three *Danzas andaluzas* (Andalusian Dances), composed in 1912.

Form: **A** = measures 1–36 (part I = 1–11; part II = 12–24; part III = 24–36); **B** = 37–77 (part I = 37–45; part II = 45–63; part III = 64–77); **A**^{1} = 78–107 (part I = 78–83; part II = 84–96; part III = 96–107).

Be sure that the 32nd notes throughout are played exactly as written and not like the third part of a triplet. Bring out the left hand in measures 1–9, 24–27, 47–48, 51–52, 78–84 and 96–99.

HEITOR VILLA-LOBOS (1887–1959)

Villa-Lobos was the first internationally recognized Brazilian composer. His music is based on folk materials using thematic idioms in a unique way. Villa-Lobos began composing in a post-Romantic style before moving to Impressionism. He later experimented with Classicism until he ultimately synthesized all of these elements.

O Polichinelo (The Punch Doll) 206

Form: **A** = measures 1–12; **A**^{1} = 13–29; **B** = 29–47; bridge = 48–50; **C** = 51–59; bridge = 60–61; coda = 62–68.

This piece comes from *A prole do bebê no. 1* (The Baby's Family), composed in 1918. Each piece is a description of one of the baby's dolls. At measures 26–44 (top voice), there is a quotation from a Brazilian folk tune, *Ciranda, Cirandinha* ("round dance, little round dance"). It suggests children joyously singing while dancing in a circle. The alternating-hands sections must be clear and precise.

Bagatelle

Béla Bartók (1881–1945)
Op. 6, No. 4; Sz. 38:4

Bear Dance

Béla Bartók (1881–1945)
Sz. 39:10

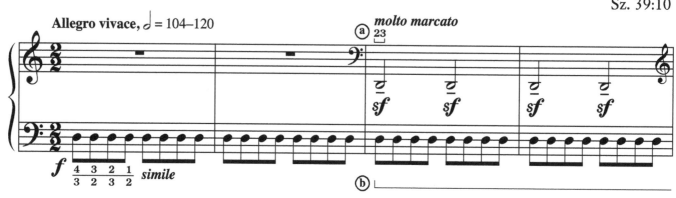

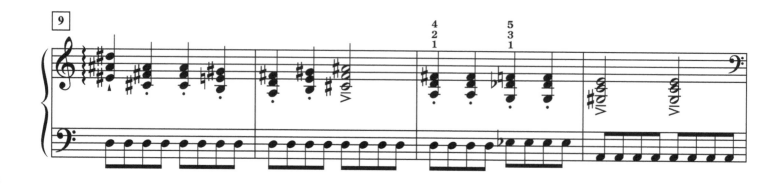

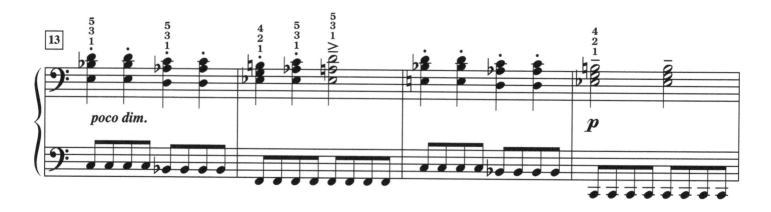

ⓐ Play low D with these two fingers.　　　　ⓑ Pedal indications are Bartók's.

Evening in the Country

Béla Bartók (1881–1945)
Sz. 39:5

ⓐ Pedal indications are Bartók's.

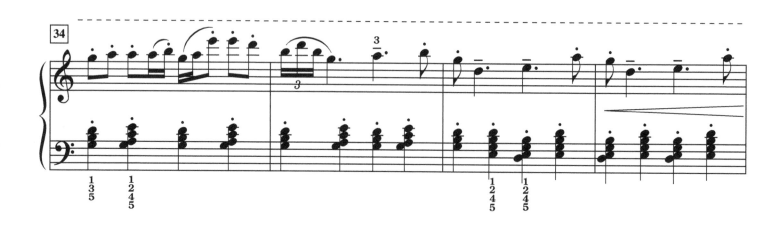

Romanian Folk Dances
Joc cu Bâtă
(Stick Dance)

Béla Bartók (1881–1945)
Sz. 56

(a) Pedal indications are Bartók's.

(b) Play all grace notes before the beat.

(c) Bartók plays a G-sharp grace note in measure 8 (like measure 32) in his Welte recording of ca. 1920.

Brâul
(Waistband Dance)

Allegro, ♩ = 134

(the 2nd time: poco ritard.)
(la 2. volta: poco ritard.)

ⓐ In his Welte recording of ca. 1920, Bartók repeats this piece, playing the right hand (with the exception of the 16th notes) in octaves.

ⓑ Pedal indications are Bartók's.

Pe loc
(On the Spot)

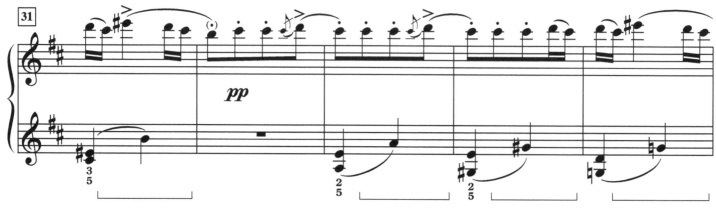

Buciumeana
(Dance of Butschum)

ⓐ Pedal indications are Bartók's. In the first edition, Bartók used pedal markings (🎹 ✻). These have been changed to line markings in this edition.

Poargă Românească
(Romanian Polka)

ⓐ Pedal indications are Bartók's except where indicated in parentheses.

ⓑ Play small notes as acciaccaturas (crushed notes) on the beat.

Măruntelul
(Lively Dance)

ⓐ Pedal indications are Bartók's.

Variations on a Slovakian Folk Tune

Béla Bartók (1881–1945)
Sz. 42:II/5

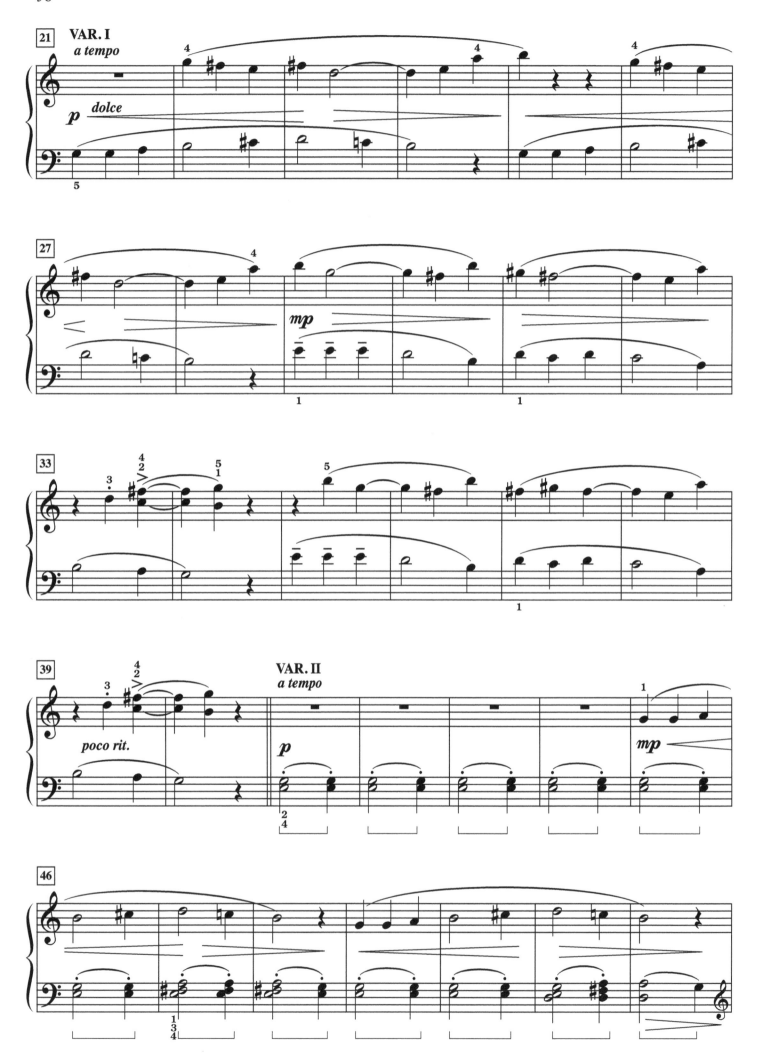

Jamaican Rumba

Arthur Benjamin
(1893–1960)

(a) Pedal indications in measures 24–26 are the composer's.

For Johnny Mehegan

Leonard Bernstein
(1918–1990)

Agitato: scherzando, ♩ = 176

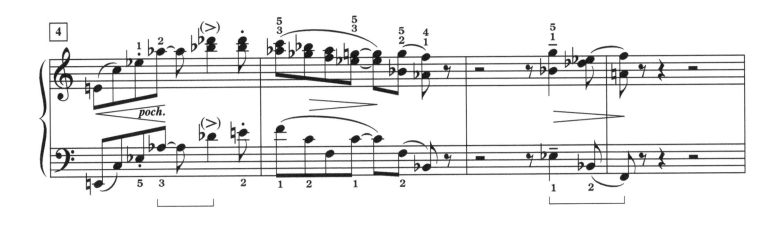

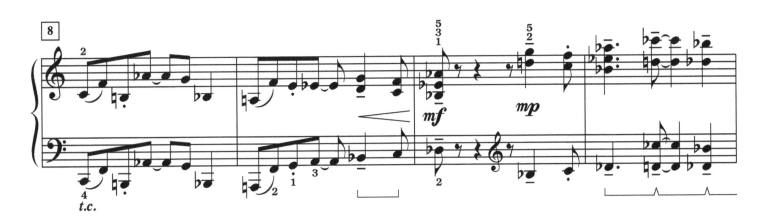

44

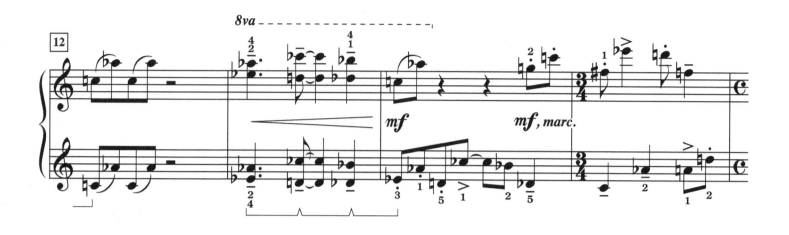

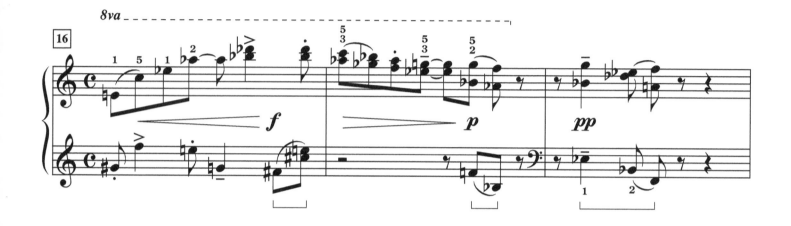

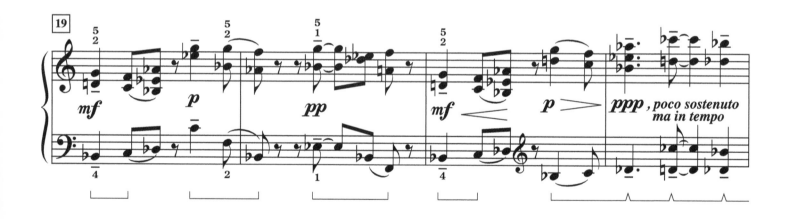

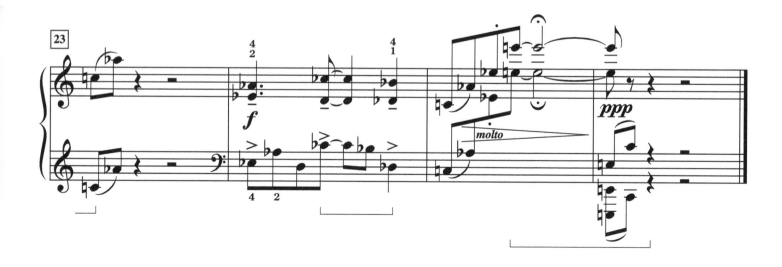

In Evening Air

"I see, in evening air,
How slowly dark comes down on what we do."
Theodore Roethke

Aaron Copland
(1900–1990)

ⓐ Fingerings are the composer's.

ⓑ Pedal indications within parentheses are editorial. All other pedal indications are the composer's.

Sentimental Melody

Aaron Copland
(1900–1990)

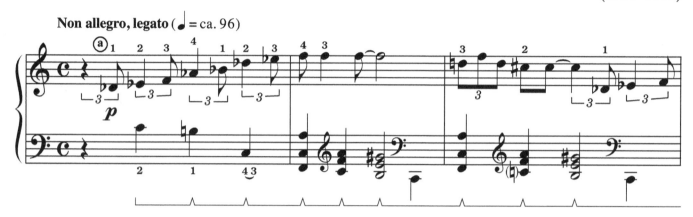

ⓐ Fingerings are the composer's.

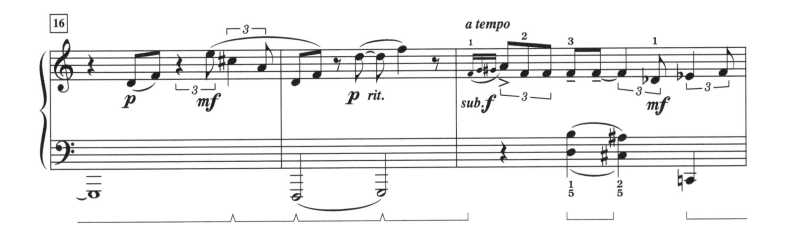

The Tides of Manaunaun
Henry Cowell

Explanation of Symbols[1]

The Symbol (a) 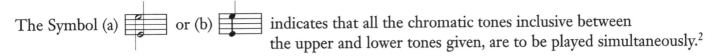 or (b) indicates that all the chromatic tones inclusive between the upper and lower tones given, are to be played simultaneously.[2]

Whole and half notes are written open, as in symbol (a).

Notes of other time values are written closed, as in symbol (b).

A sharp or flat above or below such a symbol indicates that only the black keys between the outer limits are to be played, while a natural in the same position indicates that only the white keys are to be played.

This rule is to be followed irrespective of key signature, since the tones within a tone-cluster are not affected by the key.

Only the outer tones, the highest and lowest, must be in conformance with the key signature.

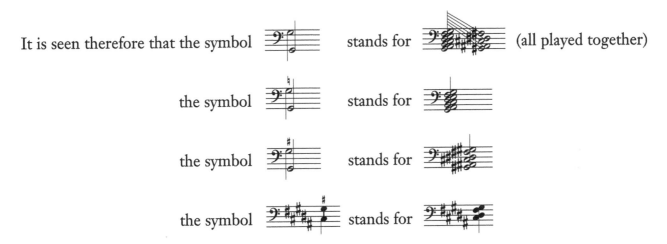

The tone clusters indicated by these symbols are to be played either with the flat of the hand, or with the forearm or with the fist, according to the length of the cluster.

Care should be taken to play all the tones exactly together, and in legato passages, to press down the keys, rather than to strike them, thus obtaining a smoother tone quality, and a unified sound.

Care must be taken that the outer limits of the clusters are absolutely precise, as written, and that each tone as indicated between the outer limits is actually sounded.

The forearm should be held in a straight line along the keys, except in case the arm of the pianist is too long, in which case the arm must be partly dropped off the keys at an angle, to give the proper length.

If desired, melody tones may be brought out with the knuckle of the little finger, in the playing of clusters.

---

[1] This explanation of symbols was written by the composer.

[2] The forearm should be placed in front of the black keys so that both the black and white keys can be depressed simultaneously.

The Tides of Manaunaun

Story according to John Varian

Manaunaun was the god of motion, and long before the creation he sent forth tremendous tides,
which swept to and fro through the universe, and rhythmically moved the particles and materials
of which the gods were later to make the suns and the worlds.

Henry Cowell
(1897–1965)

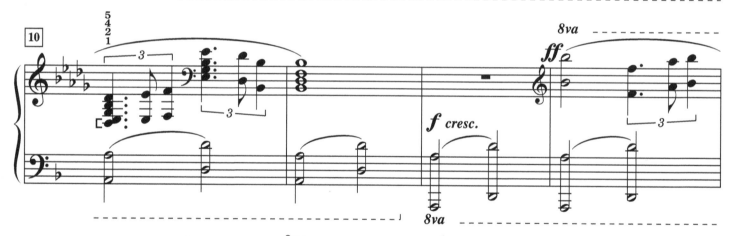

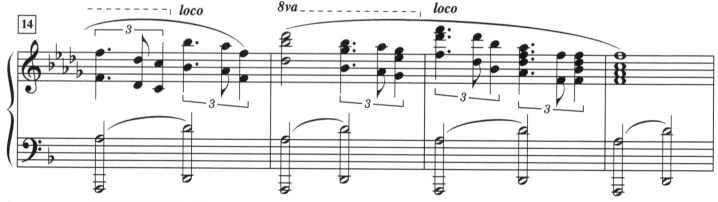

ⓐ Pedal indication is the composer's.

ⓑ Cowell's indication of *mpp* suggests a dynamic between *pp* and *p*.

Danse de la poupée

(The Doll's Dance)

Claude Debussy (1862–1918)
L. 128

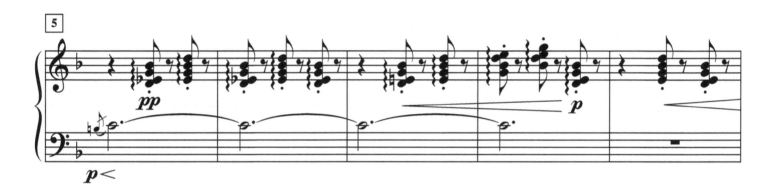

Minstrels

Claude Debussy (1862–1918)
L. 117:12

(slackening, slowing)
en cédant

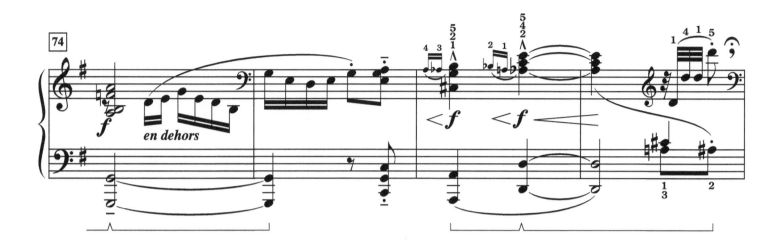

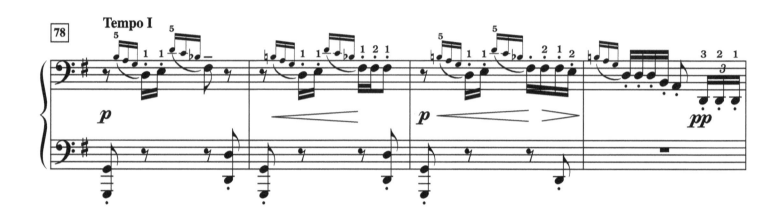

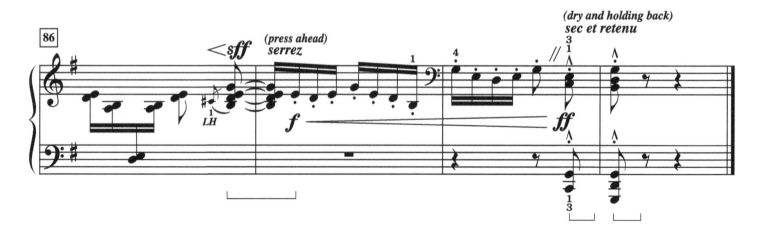

Clusters and Dots

Emma Lou Diemer
(b. 1927)

Moderately slow, clock-like (♩ = ca. 104)

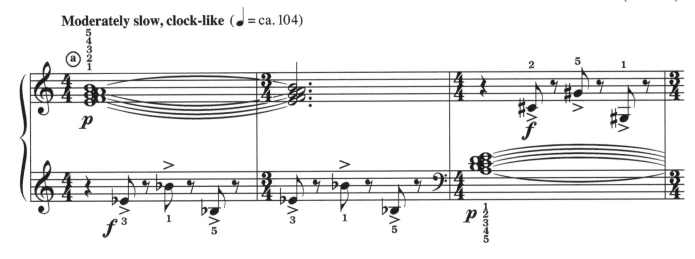

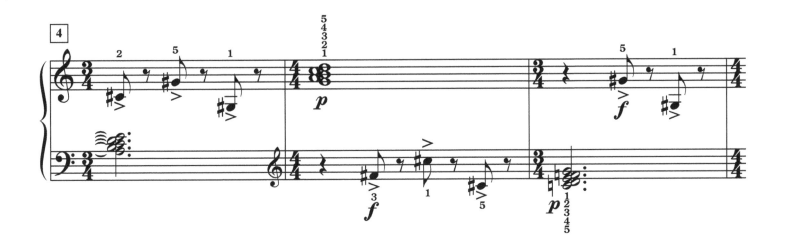

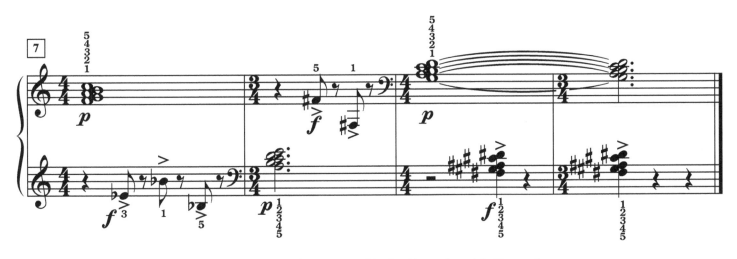

ⓐ Fingerings are the composer's.

Gigue

Emma Lou Diemer
(b. 1927)

ⓐ Fingerings are the composer's.

Serenade

Emma Lou Diemer
(b. 1927)

ⓐ Fingerings are the composer's.

Ritual Fire Dance

Manuel de Falla
(1876–1946)

(a) Editorial pedal is in parentheses. All other pedal markings are the composer's.

(b) Hold staccato half notes for approximately three-fourths of their time value (portato).

© Use both the damper and *una corda* pedals.

Approach of the Thunder God

Arthur Farwell
(1872–1952)

Medley
Campfire on the Ice

Ross Lee Finney
(1906–1997)

Chorale

Carlisle Floyd
(b. 1926)

ⓐ Fingerings are the composer's.

Fourth Lyric Piece

Carlisle Floyd
(b. 1926)

ⓐ Fingerings are the composer's.

Night Song

Carlisle Floyd
(b. 1926)

(a) Fingerings are the composer's.

(b) Pedal indications are the composer's in measures 1–4 and 7–11. All others (in parentheses) are editorial.

Waltz

Carlisle Floyd
(b. 1926)

ⓐ Fingerings are the composer's.

ⓑ Pedal indications in parentheses are editorial. Those in measures 25–32 are the composer's.

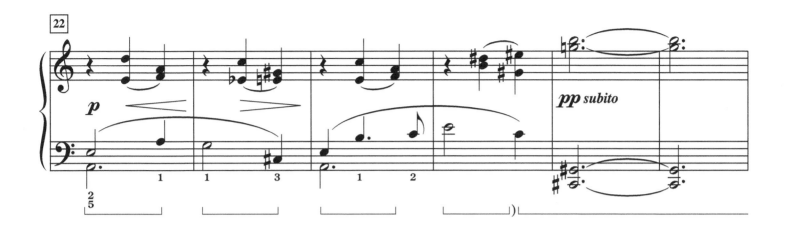

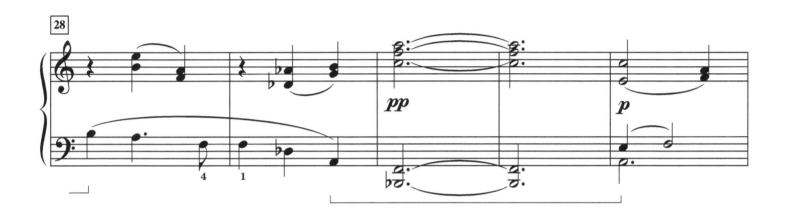

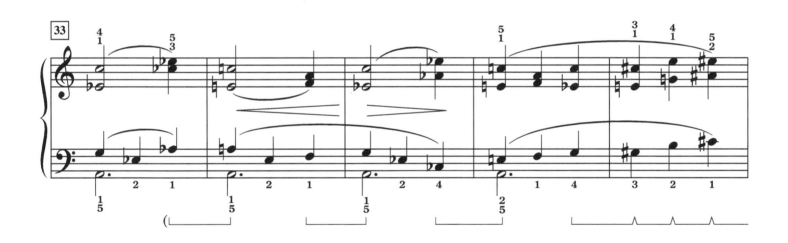

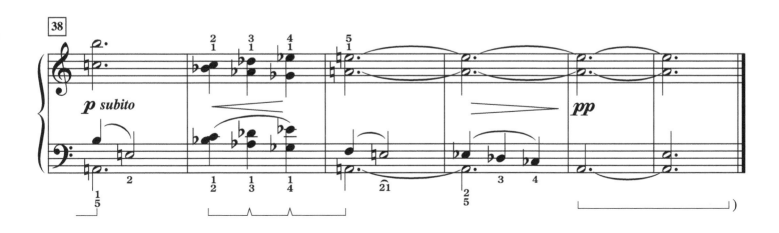

The Little Spaniard

Ignacy Friedman (1882–1948)
Op. 76, No. 7

Rondo on Argentine Children's Folk Tunes

Alberto Ginastera
(1916–1983)

Irish Tune from County Derry

Percy Grainger
(1882–1961)

The tune is thro'out printed in bigger notes ⓐ

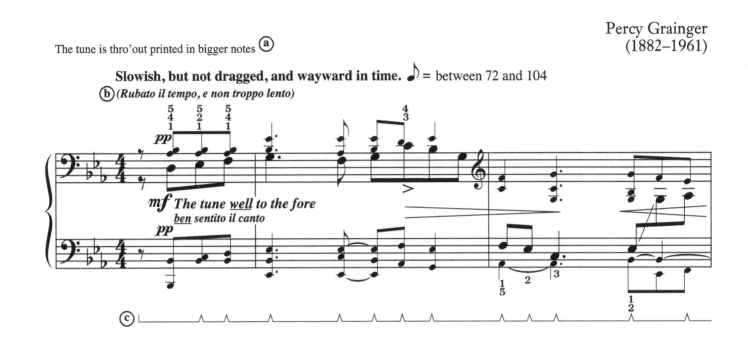

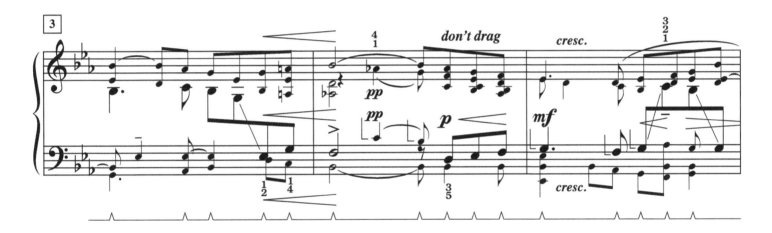

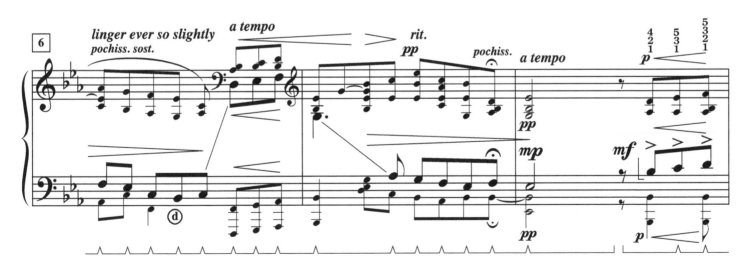

ⓐ This indication comes from Grainger.

ⓑ All parentheses in this piece are Grainger's.

ⓒ Pedal markings are Grainger's.

ⓓ Grainger wrote the following note in the score: "This note (here altered by me) is B-natural in the original."

ⓔ The sign ✳ indicates a pedal change for the sostenuto pedal.

ⓕ Grainger wrote the following note in the score: "If you like, the passage between * and ** [in measures 16–20] may be played an octave higher (in both hands)."

ⓖ Grainger wrote the following note in the score: "This note (here altered by me) is B-natural in the original."

The Sussex Mummer's Christmas Carol

Percy Grainger
(1882–1961)

The tune, printed in big notes, should be brought out with a rich, piercing tone
and heard well above the accompanying parts. ⓐ

Slowish, but flowing, ♪ = between 84 and 100

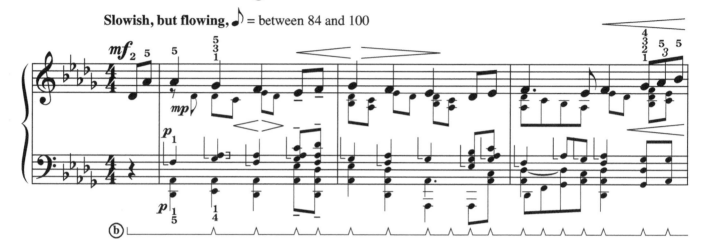

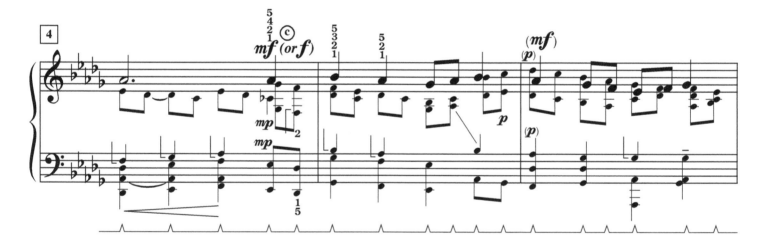

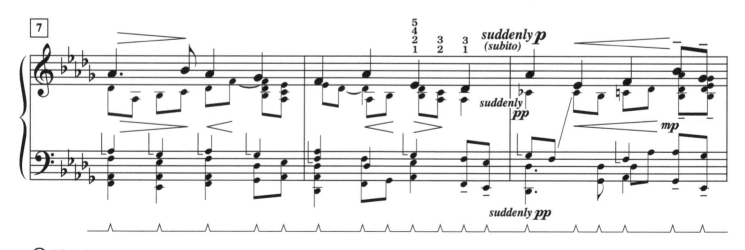

ⓐ This direction comes from Grainger.

ⓑ Pedal markings are Grainger's.

ⓒ All parentheses in this piece are Grainger's.

ⓓ Grainger wrote the following note in the score: "The rhythm of these two notes is here altered by me. The original form is given in the first time through [measure 9]."

The White Peacock

Charles Griffes (1884–1920)
Op. 7, No. 1

(a) Added security is gained by striking the C-sharp with both fingers simultaneously.

The Lake at Evening

. . . for always. . .
I hear lake water lapping with low sounds
by the shore. . . .

William Butler Yeats
from *The Lake Isle of Innisfree*

Charles Griffes (1884–1920)
Op. 5, No. 1

ⓐ Pedal indications are the composer's.

(b) Arpeggiate the downstem notes before the beat, and play the upstem F-sharp on the beat.

Reel

Homage to Henry Cowell

Lou Harrison
(1917–2003)

(a) The large sharp on the treble staff indicates that all notes are to be sharped (played on black keys). The large natural sign on the bass staff indicates that all notes are to be natural (played on white keys) unless accidentals are used.

(b) All dynamics are editorial.

(c) In playing these *palm clusters*, the two outer notes should be slightly louder than the interior ones.

ⓓ In playing these half-arm clusters, the little finger of the fist should strongly bring out the lowest note.

(repeat with octave
in bass tune)

ⓔ The unconnected "ties" are not actually ties. Rather, they are an indication to let the notes ring.

A Giddy Girl

Jacques Ibert
(1890–1962)

ⓐ Pedal indications in measures 1–2 and 9–10 are the composer's. Those in parentheses are editorial.

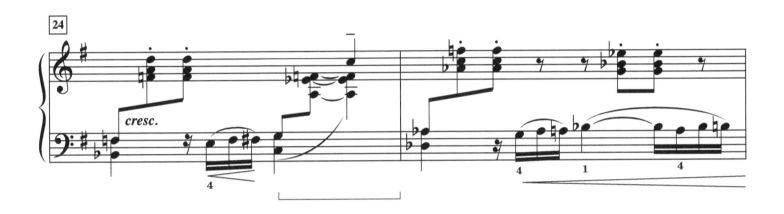

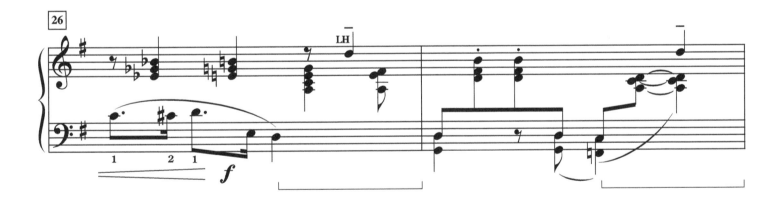

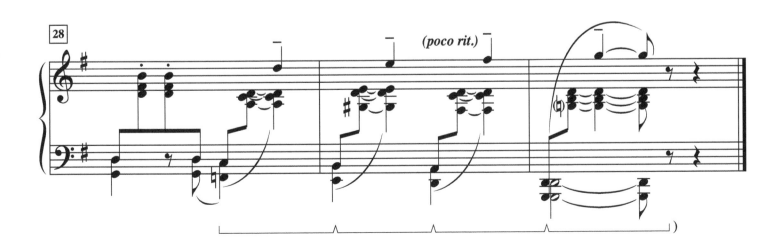

Three Love Songs

Gently, Johnny, My Jingalo

Nelson Keyes
(1928–1987)

Shenandoah

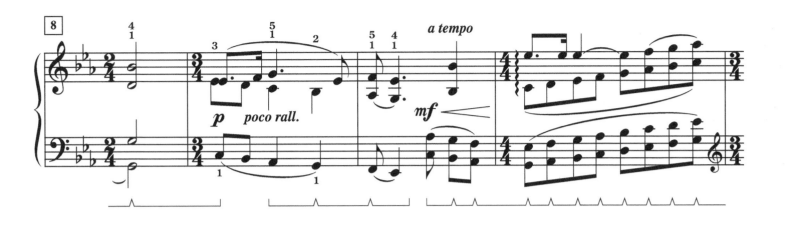

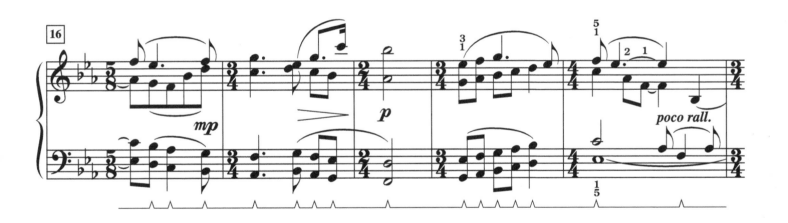

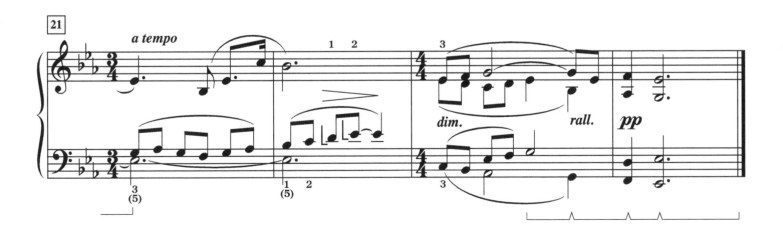

Lolly-Too-Dum

Young People's Dance
for the Black Keys

Zoltán Kodály
(1882–1967)

ⓐ The large sharps indicate that all notes are to be sharped (played on black keys).

ⓑ The A in parentheses is optional.

Ⓒ The wedge-shaped *staccatissimos* should be played shorter than staccato.

Kaleidoscopes
No. 9

Benjamin Lees
(b. 1924)

No. 10

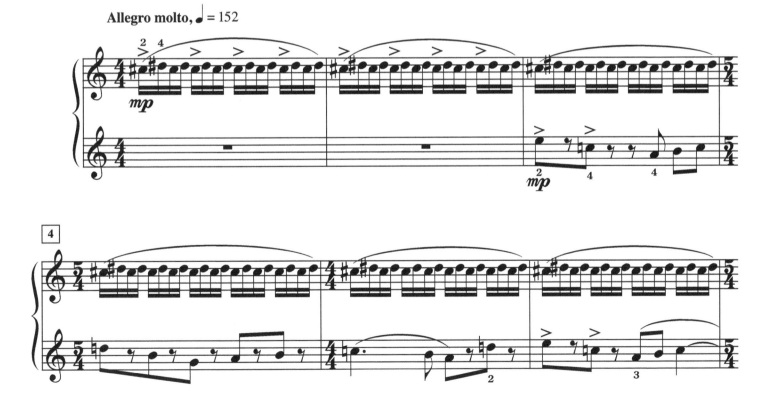

Columbine Dances

Waltz

Bohuslav Martinů
(1890–1959)

ⓐ Pedal indications and fingerings are the composer's.

Tempo I

The New Puppet

Shimmy

Bohuslav Martinů
(1890–1959)

ⓐ Fingerings are the composer's.

ⓑ This pedal indication is the composer's.

(A little more lively)
Poco vivo

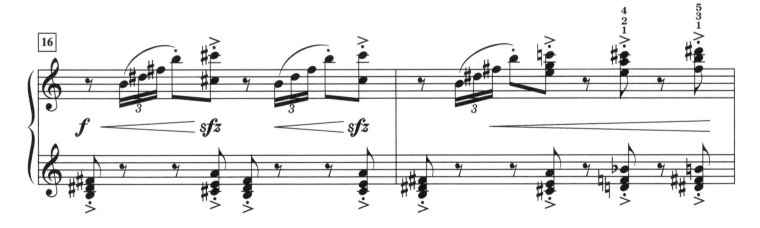

134

(Still a little more lively)
Ancora poco più vivo

Tempo I

The Shy Doll
Chanson

Bohuslav Martinů
(1890–1959)

(a) Pedal indications and fingerings are the composer's.

Sorocaba

Darius Milhaud (1892–1974)
Op. 67, No. 1

139

for Madame Régis de Oliveira

(a) The unconnected "ties" are not actually ties. Rather, they are an indication to let the notes ring.

Mouvement perpétuels
No. 1

Francis Poulenc
(1899–1963)

(Rather moderately)
Assez modéré, ♩ = 144

En général, sans nuances
(In general, without nuances)

(bring out)
mf **en dehors**

(gently, but lightly stressed)
p **doucement timbré**

ⓐ Grace notes in measures 10, 14–17 and 24 are played before the beat.

(b) Poulenc indicated to hold the pedal for the entire measure.

No. 2

(a) Grace notes in measures 5, 7, 9 and 11–12 are played before the beat.
(b) Composer's pedal indication.
(c) Play the glissando with these three fingers.

144

No. 3

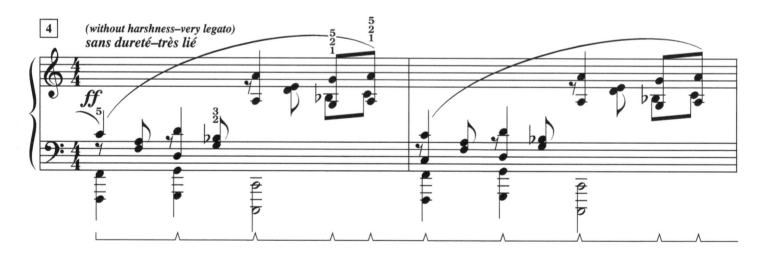

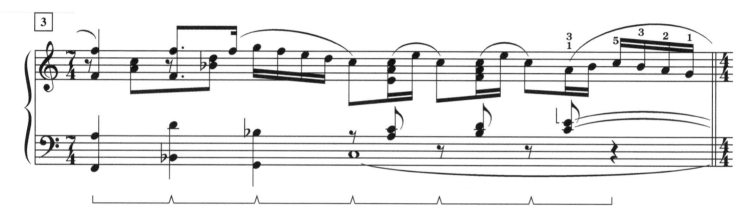

ⓐ The repeat bar is editorial.

ⓑ The unconnected "ties" are not actually ties. Rather, they are an indication to let the notes ring.
They can be found in measures 2, 3, 38, 39 and 57.

ⓒ Grace notes in measures 15, 31, 33, 35, 42 and 49–50 are played before the beat.

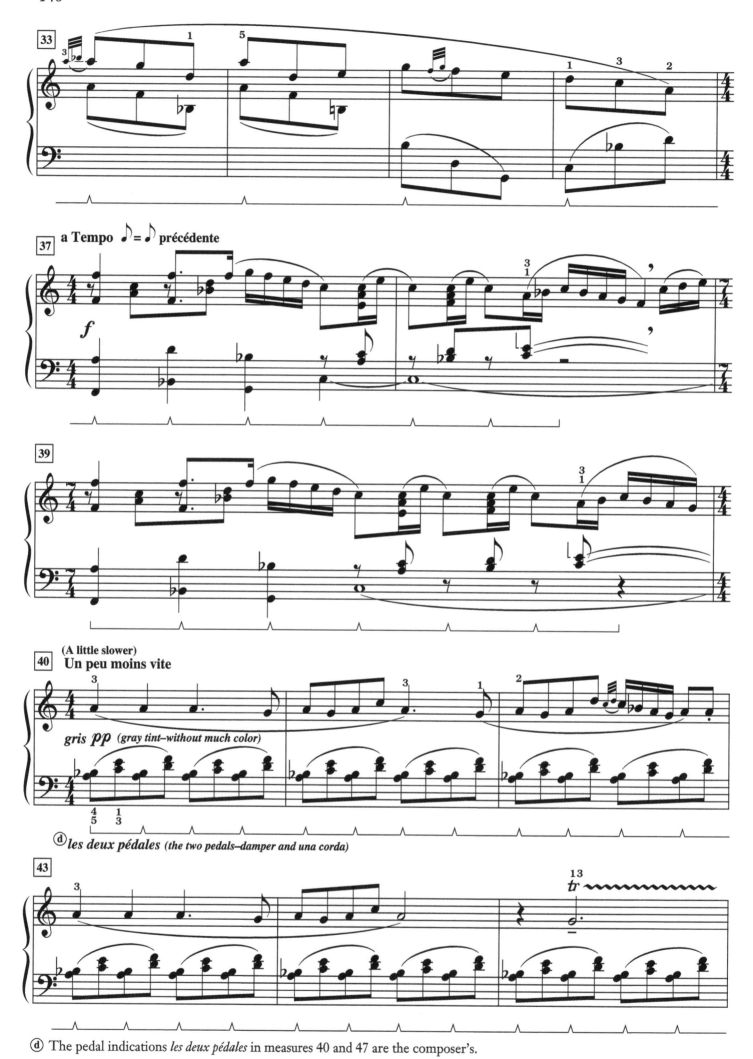

ⓓ The pedal indications *les deux pédales* in measures 40 and 47 are the composer's.

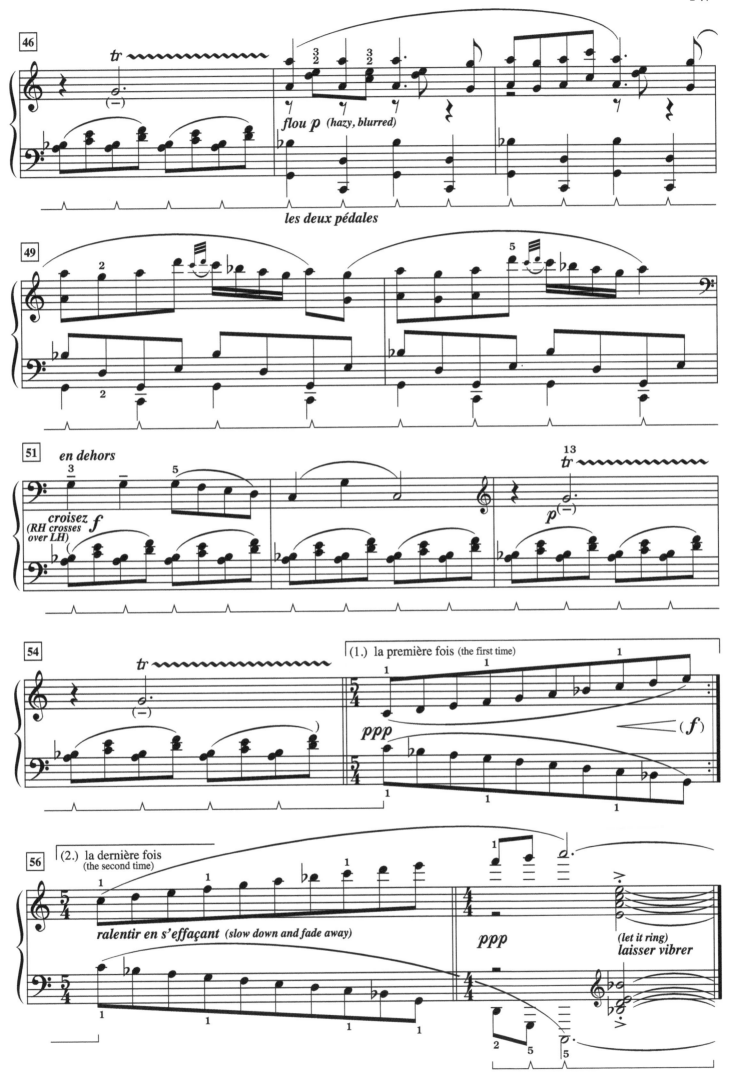

February 15

André Previn
(b. 1929)

Prelude in C Major
("Harp")

Serge Prokofiev (1891–1953)
Op. 12, No. 7

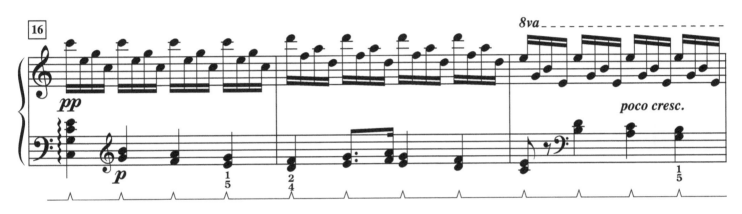

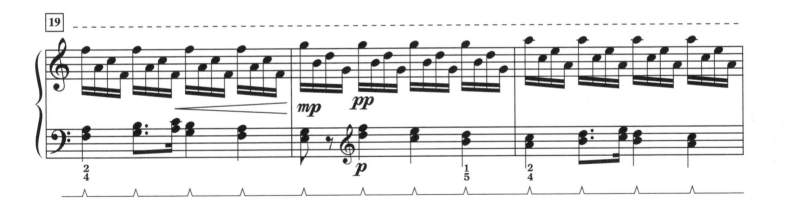

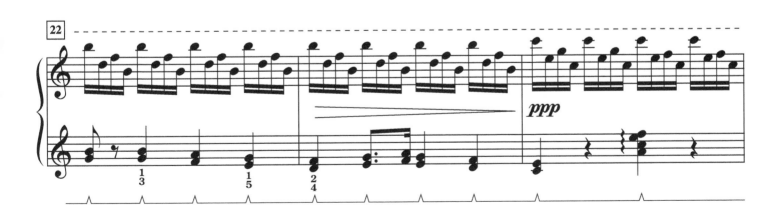

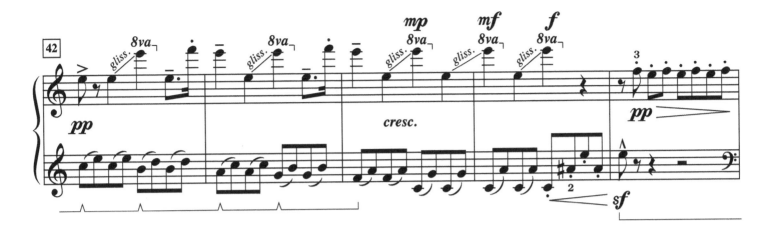

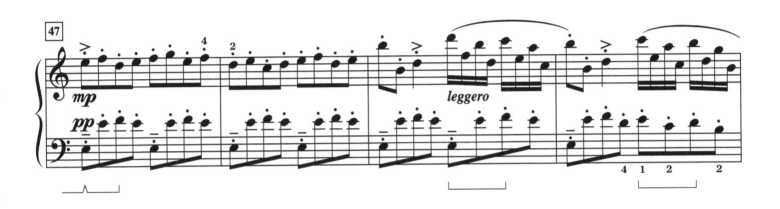

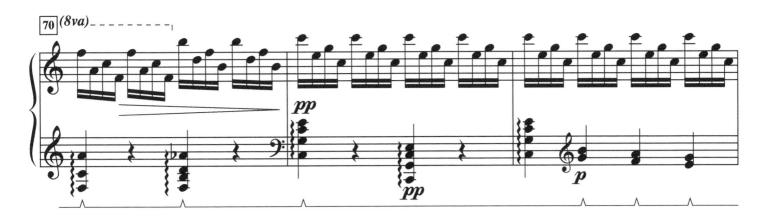

Visions Fugitives
No. 1

Serge Prokofiev (1891–1953)
Op. 22

No. 5

ⓐ Pedal indication is the composer's.

À la manière de Borodin

(In the Style of Borodin)

Valse

Maurice Ravel
(1875–1937)

Prélude

(Rather slowly and very expressive– rhythmically free)
Assez lent et très expressif (d'un rythme libre), ♩ = 60 **environ** (approximately)

Maurice Ravel
(1875–1937)

ⓐ Ravel gave only two pedal indications: the first, 𝕻𝖊𝖉. in measure 2 (simply to indicate pedal in the piece); the second in measure 20 beginning under the left-hand part, continuing to a release on the second beat of measure 22. All other pedal is editorial.

ⓑ At measures 10–15, keep the left hand raised considerably above the right.

Dancing Demons

Vladimir Rebikov
(1866–1920)

Sad Moment

Vladimir Rebikov
(1866–1920)

The Augmented Triad

Wallingford Riegger
(1885–1961)

ⓐ Indication in parentheses is the composer's.

The Major Second

Wallingford Riegger
(1885–1961)

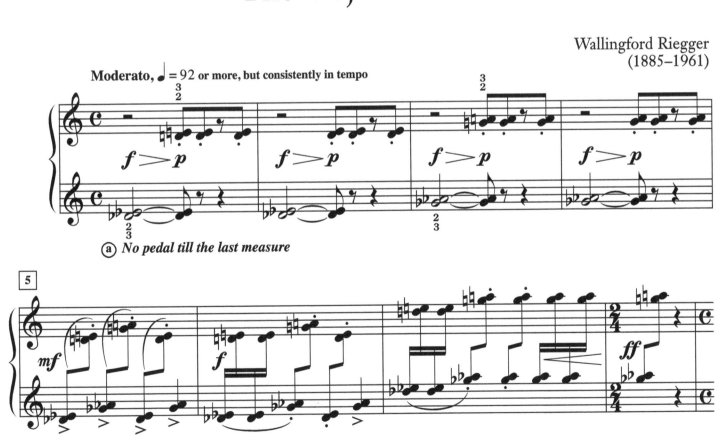

ⓐ Pedal indications are the composer's.

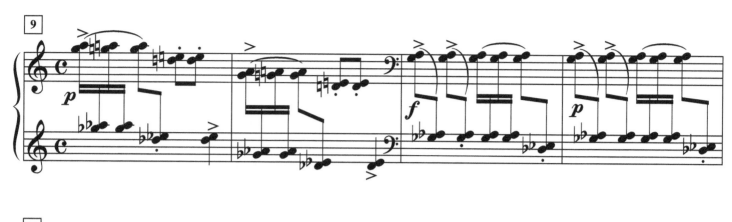

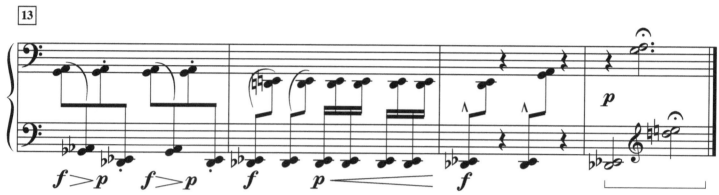

The Tritone

Fast, but not at the expense of clarity, $\dotminim = 100$

Wallingford Riegger
(1885–1961)

Le Piccadilly
Marche

Erik Satie
(1866–1925)

ⓐ The unconnected "ties" are not actually ties. Rather, they are an indication to let the notes ring.

Sonatine bureaucratique

(Bureaucratic Sonatina)

Erik Satie
(1866–1925)

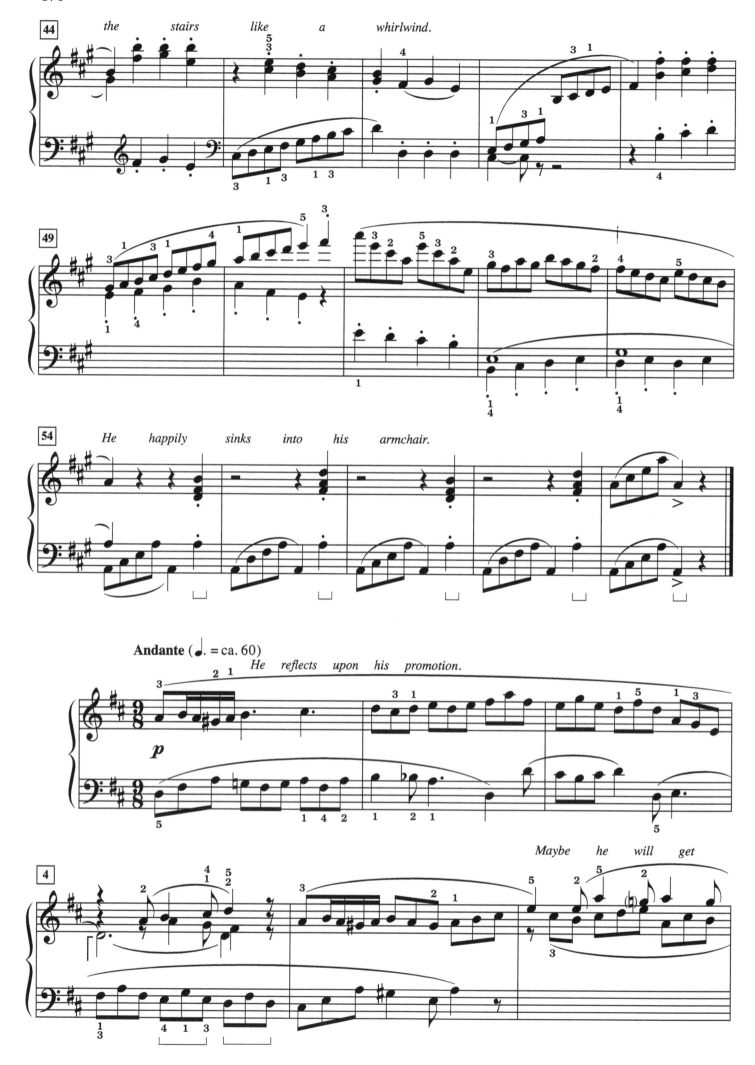

Six Little Piano Pieces
No. 2

Arnold Schoenberg (1874–1951)
Op. 19

No. 6

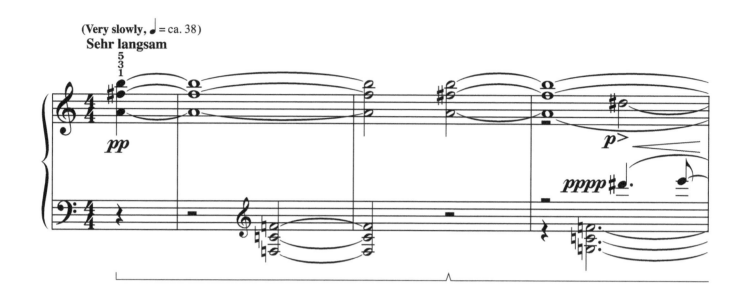

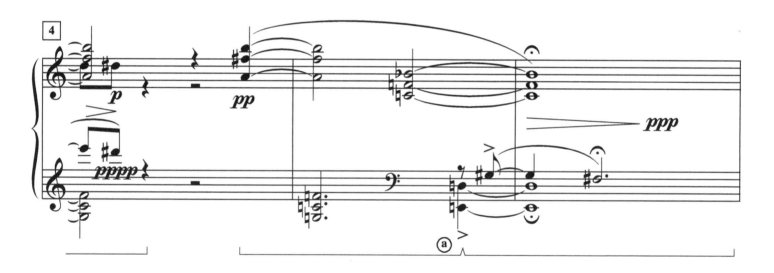

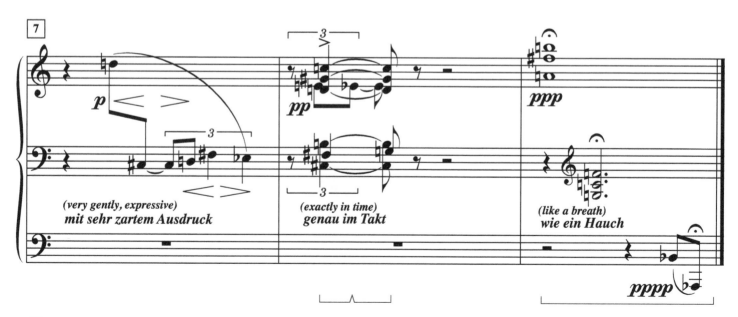

ⓐ The composer indicated pedal starting on beat 4 of measure 5, held through measure 6.

Lento
No. 2

Cyril Scott (1879–1970)
Op. 35, No. 1

ⓐ For all arpeggiated chords throughout, begin the arpeggio before the beat, allowing the top note to be played on the beat.

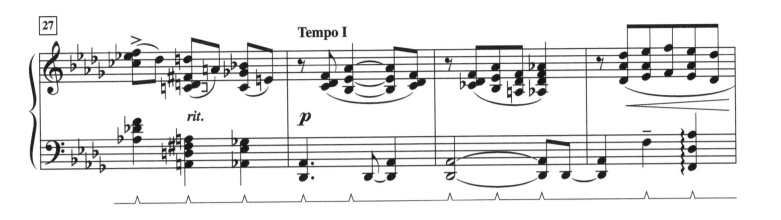

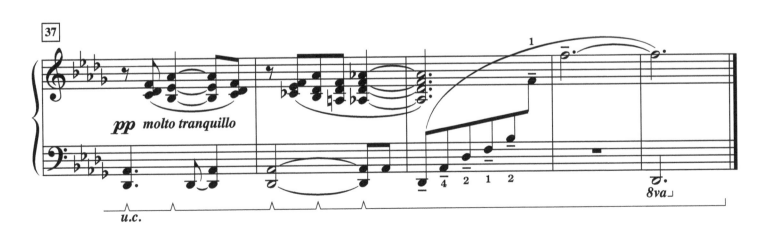

Siciliana ⓐ

Igor Stravinsky
(1882–1971)

ⓐ Title is editorial.

ⓑ Articulation is editorial.

ⓒ All dynamics are editorial.

Lento

Igor Stravinsky
(1882–1971)

Ⓐ All dynamics are editorial.

Pesante

Igor Stravinsky
(1882–1971)

(a) All dynamics are editorial.

Prelude in B Minor

Karol Szymanowski (1882–1937)
Op. 1, No. 1

Ten Bagatelles
No. 1

Alexander Tcherepnin (1899–1977)
Op. 5

ⓐ The wedge-shaped *staccatissimos* should be played shorter than staccato.

No. 9

Homage to Marya Freund and to the Harp

Virgil Thomson
(1896–1989)

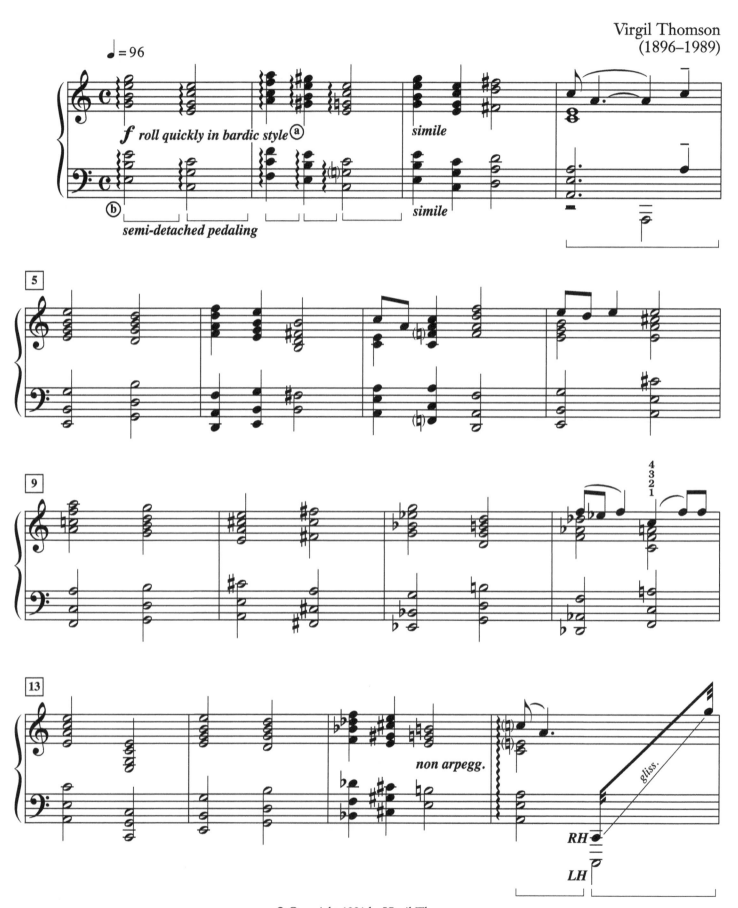

ⓐ This direction refers to the quick, light arpeggiations of a Celtic harpist.

ⓑ Pedal markings are Thomson's.

Sam Byers: With Joy

Virgil Thomson
(1896–1989)

Tango

Joaquín Turina (1882–1949)
Op. 8, No. 2

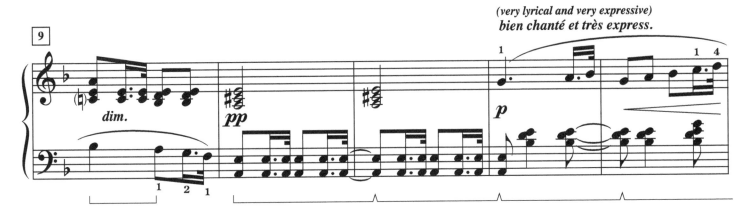

ⓐ Play the arpeggiated chords in measures 37, 93 and 94 before the beat,
with the top note of the chord sounding on the downbeat.

204

O Polichinelo

Heitor Villa-Lobos
(1887–1959)

col pedal sempre ⓐ

ⓐ This indication is the composer's.

(bring out the melody)
le chant bien distinct

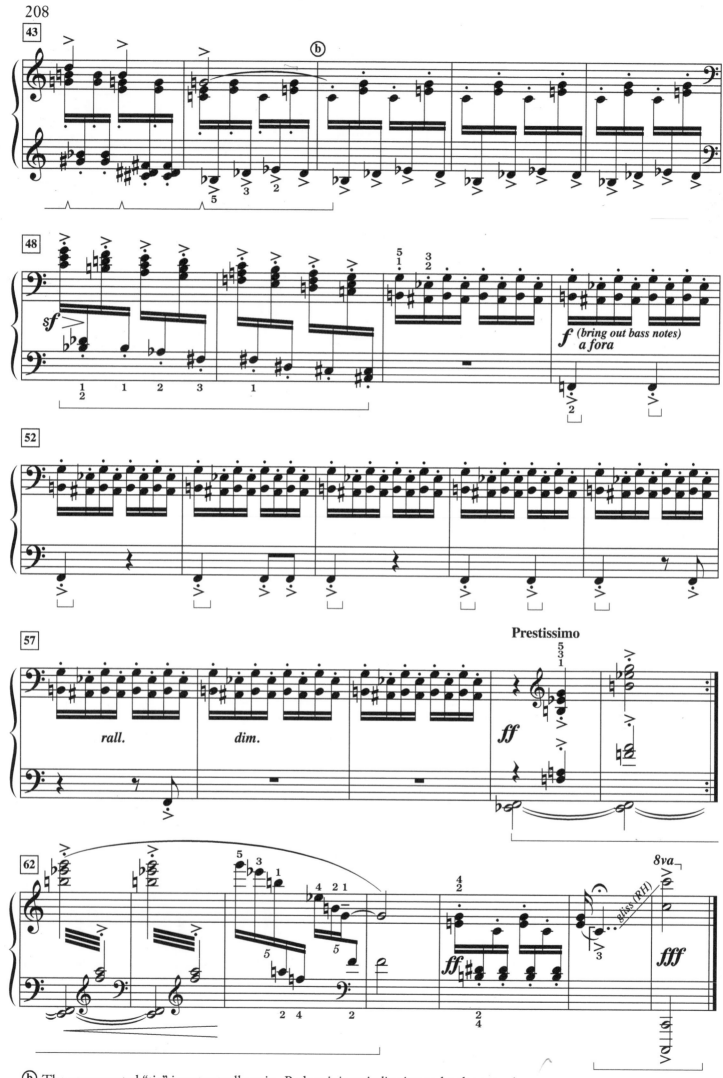

ⓑ The unconnected "tie" is not actually a tie. Rather, it is an indication to let the note ring.